ENTERTAINING
Island Style

101 Great Recipes and Tips from Hawai'i

Wanda A. Adams

Published and distributed by

ISLAND HERITAGE™
P U B L I S H I N G
A DIVISION OF THE MADDEN CORPORATION

94-411 KŌ'AKI STREET, WAIPAHU, HAWAI'I 96797-2806
ORDERS: (800) 468-2800
INFORMATION: (808) 564-8800
FAX: (808) 564-8877
islandheritage.com

ISBN# : 1-59700-522-3
Second Edition, Second Printing - 2012

Cover Background Photography by Susan Benay
Food Photography by Roméo S. Collado, unless otherwise noted.
Food styled by Iwa Bush and Chris Jose.

DEDICATION

For Marylene Chun, a food friend, a true friend.

ACKNOWLEDGEMENTS

The author and publisher extend a *mahalo piha* (big thank you) to the Westye Group-West in Honolulu,
distributors of Sub-Zero and Wolf appliances, and to Jean Nakanishi and chef Carol Nardello for the use of
their beautiful (and beautifully equipped) kitchen showroom for the food photography in this book.

Warmest *mahalos* to corporate chef Keoni Chang and the STAFF at Foodland,
and to chef-restaurateur Raymond Siu of Pah Ke's Chinese Restaurant in Kāneʻohe.

About the Author

Veteran food writer Wanda A. Adams, a Maui native of Portuguese descent, has a deep interest in the history of Island foods. Her first book, *The Island Plate: 150 Years of Recipes and Food Lore from The Honolulu Advertiser*, sold out in two editions. Wanda and her husband, Carl E. "Sonny" Koonce, live in Kapālama, Oʻahu, with their cats, Precious, Popoki, and Paʻi. Contact her at idasylva@clearwire.com.

©IHP Archive

Contents

E komo mai! Come in!

Islanders are a welcoming people, and food is our language of hospitality—an Island party is considered successful when there is three times as much food as can be consumed!

We are an informal culture, but that doesn't mean we lack rules. The rules are: you always bring something, and you must always take something away.

Read on to understand the Island way of entertaining.

He ʻai leo ʻole, he ʻīpuka hāmama.
Food unaccompanied by a voice; a door always open.

A saying indicative of the tradition of Hawaiian hospitality: you are welcome even if no one is there; come in and make yourself at home.

–*ʻŌlelo Noʻeau Hawaiian Proverbs and Poetical Sayings*, by Mary Kawena Pukui (Bishop Museum Press, 1983)

Ingredient Notes

Here are some tidbits on ingredients that will help you make the most of your Island-style culinary efforts. Note that the glossary at the end contains definitions of ingredients that may be unfamiliar to you. In addition, wherever possible, substitutes are indicated for ingredients that may be difficult to locate outside of Hawai'i.

Boned chicken thighs: these are the centerpieces for dozens of popular Island dishes. If thighs aren't readily available boned where you live, you can easily do it yourself: using a sharp boning knife, cut along the thinner inside of the thigh and along the length of the bone; hold one end of bone and scrape meat down while turning bone; chop off end cartilage.

Ginger: Unless specified, the ginger called for in these recipes is fresh ginger, which must be peeled (with a vegetable peeler or sharp knife) and minced or grated, just like garlic. Dried ginger spice has a distinctly different flavor.

The best way to grate ginger is with a Japanese-style porcelain grater (*shoga oroshi*) especially designed for this purpose. Peeled ginger is rubbed in a circular motion over a grating surface comprised of needle-sharp points. A surrounding indentation acts like a moat to capture the ginger juice. As an alternative, you can use a micro plane rasp or the finest holes of a conventional grater.

Hawaiian salt: Contrary to what you may have been told, Hawaiian salt is generally not naturally harvested from seawater. It's a commercially manufactured granular salt similar to kosher salt, which is also the best substitute for Hawaiian salt. *'Alaea*, a salt preferred by many Islanders, is mixed with red clay.

©iStockphoto.com/Diane Rutt

Peppers: The most popular chile in Hawai'i is a small, very hot, red pepper about the length, and slightly less than the width, of your little finger. It is universally referred to as "Hawaiian chile pepper," or *nīoi*. Thai bird chiles can be substituted.

Rice: White rice, most commonly the Calrose variety of medium-grain rice, is the starch of choice for the people of the Islands. While most rice today is no longer treated with starch, it is still common to wash rice by rinsing it several times in cold water. Rinsing the rice, while unnecessary for safety reasons, does start the process of tenderizing the rice grain. Rice is steamed in a Japanese rice cooker (one part rice to one part water) or on the stovetop (one part rice to two parts water). When cooking rice on a stovetop, boil water; add rice; and cover. Turn heat down to low; then, allow to steam 20 minutes.

Soy sauce: Except when specified, use Hawaiian soy sauce (such as Aloha Shoyu, in its low-sodium version), which is milder and sweeter than Japanese versions. When I use Japanese soy sauce, I prefer the low-sodium Yamasa brand. While substituting another soy sauce won't make an immense difference, it will certainly be detectable to those knowledgeable about local flavors.

©iStockphoto.com/Andrea Velez-Greene

©iStockphoto.com/Claudio Baldini

10

Wasabi: The amount of this Japanese horseradish you use depends on the type. Powdered or tube-paste wasabi (which isn't real wasabi) is rather hot, but is subtle in flavor, so you'll need to use more of these types. Fresh wasabi (if you can find it—and afford it at $80 to $100 per pound) should be peeled and grated finely, and added with a judicious hand.

Watercress: Island watercress is long and leggy, with foot-long stems. Mainland watercress is much shorter, with more delicate stems. Standard practice in the Islands is to blanch watercress in boiling water, then wring out the moisture before using watercress in dishes. This technique is not necessary with the watercress found on the U.S. mainland.

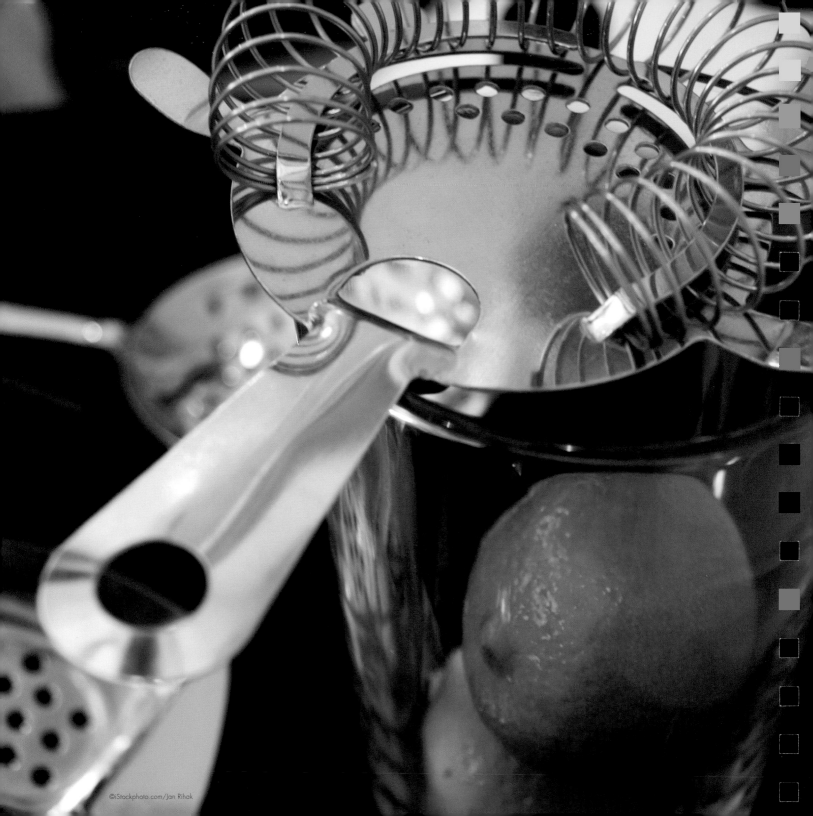

'Ōkole Maluna is the Island way to say "bottoms up." In truth, most Islanders drank beer and soda until recent years, when both wine and cocktails gained popularity—tropical drinks were considered a "tourist thing." Now, with the rebirth of the cocktail, we've become proud of our mixological skills and Hawai'i's place in drink history.

Equipment:

In addition to the jigger, bottle opener, and corkscrew that are essential for any home bar, these additional items should also be included.

* Cocktail shaker (glass bottom, stainless steel top)
* Hawthorne strainer (that funny-looking round thing with the coil of wire around the edge)
* Muddler (wooden or plastic pestle used to bruise ingredients to release the flavorful esters)
* Citrus reamer and sharp paring knife, as well as a citrus stripper or zester

Tips:

Ice: Clean, fresh ice is vital to proper bartending. Make both cubes and cracked or shaved ice fresh from bottled water. To crack ice, place cubes in a zippered plastic bag (freezer strength is best), cover with a cloth towel, place on a cutting board, and then have at them with a rolling pin or mallet.

Chilling glasses: Note that many cocktail recipes suggest chilling the glass first, which can be done in the refrigerator, but is also effectively achieved by filling the glass with ice cubes or cracked ice while you assemble the drink ingredients in a cocktail mixer. Pour out the chilling ice and add new ice before straining the drink into the glass. If you're a fanatic about fancy drinks you can buy an ice-shaving machine, but it's not a necessity.

Shaken or stirred? James Bond was wrong (gasp!). *Shake* drinks that should be light and frothy—as with fruity or creamy drinks. *Stir* drinks made with clear spirits to avoid diluting the drink too much.

15

Poi Cocktail

1 c. half-and-half (nonfat is fine)

4 oz. bourbon or other whiskey

⅛ tsp. salt

2 tsp. fine sugar

4 Tbsp. fresh, thin poi

Nutmeg or cinnamon for garnish (optional)

Chill two martini glasses by filling with crushed ice. In a blender, combine half-and-half, whiskey, salt, sugar, and poi. Blend until combined. Add a handful of crushed ice; blend briefly. Discard ice from glasses; fill glasses with cocktail.

Serves 2

©IHP Archive

The poi cocktail was the "in" drink among Island elite in the early twentieth century, probably to make the best of an abundance of poi and a lack of more familiar cocktail ingredients. But the term encompasses a wide range of drinks, from alcohol-free concoctions to nourish babies to potent libations made with bourbon or brandy.

At its simplest, a poi cocktail is merely a mix of young poi (one- or two-day poi, not soured by fermentation), milk, and crushed or shaved ice bolstered with a dash of salt and/or sugar. Other versions use cream, half-and-half (or even ice cream), and various flavorings, from vanilla to cinnamon.

Mai Tai

Juice of 1 lime

¼ oz. orange curacao

¼ oz. orgeat syrup

2 oz. pineapple juice

1 oz. light rum

1 oz. dark rum

Lime wedge, paper umbrella, Vanda orchid for garnish (optional)

Fill double old-fashioned glass with crushed ice; set aside to chill. In cocktail shaker, combine lime juice, curaçao, orgeat, and pineapple juice. Shake. Pour over crushed ice, then layer rums: first light, then dark. Garnish with Vanda orchid and paper umbrella stuck into lime wedge.

Serves 1

The mai tai—that quintessential Island cocktail—actually came from California. With whom? Ah, that is the question.

Don the Beachcomber (Ernest Raymond Beaumont Gantt–who later legally changed his name to Donn Beach) claimed he concocted the drink in 1934 in Hollywood at his original Don's Beachcomber restaurant. After traveling extensively in the Caribbean, he developed an appreciation for fine rum, which he parlayed into a bar and restaurant career that spanned the Pacific.

However, well-known restaurateur Trader Vic (Victor Jules Bergeron Jr.) insisted he invented the drink in 1944. Its name, he said, came from a Tahitian friend who responded to the invention by exclaiming, "mai tai," which Vic translated as "out of this world." The proper Tahitian word is *maita'i*, which corresponds precisely to the Hawaiian word *maika'i*, meaning "good." Trader Vic wrote that he brought the drink to Hawai'i in 1953 when he was designing drinks for the Matson Steamship Lines hotels, including the Royal Hawaiian—the site of the Mai Tai Bar, which also claims to be the site of the drink's invention!

What's the truth? No one can say. But this rum and fruit juice drink has become a bar standard associated with Hawai'i. My husband's recipe here is less sweet than some—he uses pineapple juice rather than orange and omits the sugar syrup used in many versions.

19

Pomegranate in Paradise

1 oz. tequila (Patron Silver Tequila, if available)

¼ oz. orange-flavored liqueur (Cointreau, if available)

3 oz. pomegranate juice

⅛ slice of fresh lime

Kosher salt, lime wedge for garnish

©iStockphoto.com/Kelly Cline

Fill cocktail mixer to top with ice. Pour in tequila, orange-flavored liqueur, and pomegranate juice. Squeeze in generous slice of fresh lime. Secure mixer top; shake vigorously. Pour contents into wineglass rimmed with kosher salt. Garnish with lime wedge.

Serves 1

Dr. Joey's Shanghai Diva

1 whole fresh, ripe strawberry

1 tsp. sugar (or to taste)

1 oz. strawberry vodka, (Stoli Strasberi, if available)

Crushed ice

Superfine granulated sugar (colored, if desired)

In cocktail shaker, place strawberry and sugar. Muddle sugar and strawberry together to form a paste. Add strawberry vodka and fill to top with crushed ice. Secure stainless steel top on shaker. Shake in classic bartender's up-and-down motion until fully incorporated. Strain into chilled, sugar-rimmed martini glass.

Serves 1

At E&O Trading Co. in Honolulu, Joey Gottesman, working under the "nom-de-bar" of Dr. Joey, created this self-proclaimed "lounge elixir."

Carthaginian's Downfall

1 oz. rum (Meyer's, if available)

¼ oz. Galliano (an Italian herbal liqueur)

¼ oz. orange-flavored liqueur (Cointreau, if available)

½ oz. crème de noyaux (a blush-colored, almond-flavored liqueur
   made from fruit pits)

½ oz. light crème de cacao

2 oz. orange juice

2 oz. pineapple juice

Crushed ice

No Cointreau?
Use triple-sec.

No crème de noyaux?
Use orgeat syrup.

Place all ingredients in cocktail shaker with a couple of ice cubes. Shake. Pour over crushed ice in a chimney (a tall 14-ounce glass also known as a Collins glass) or in double old-fashioned glass.

Serves 1

©iStockphoto.com/Tomo Jesenicnik

My husband, Sonny, a bartender for twenty years, invented this drink in 1972 while working at the popular Rusty Harpoon Bar at Whalers Village in Ka'anapali. His inspiration was the sinking of the Carthaginian, a wooden-hulled barge built for the movie *Hawaii*, which, while headed to an O'ahu dry dock for maintenance, was snagged on a reef off Lahaina Harbor. Rumor had it that drinking was involved in the ship's demise. In any case, Sonny commemorated this event with a concoction he named Carthaginian's Downfall.

The Fifth Element

3 oz. fresh seedless watermelon, chopped

1 whole fresh ripe strawberry

Juice of 1 fresh ripe orange

Orange slice and mint sprig for garnish

In mixing glass of a cocktail shaker, combine watermelon and strawberry. Muddle thoroughly, macerating as much juice as possible. Add orange juice, then fill to top with ice. Strain into chilled wineglass filled with fresh ice. Garnish with orange slice and mint.

Serves 1

This is a great nonalcoholic summer beverage. (If you prefer, you can add a jigger of vodka.) Mixologist Joey, "Dr. Joey," Gottesman makes this drink with orchard-ripened Kona oranges. These oranges aren't pretty, but they are wonderfully sweet and tart. (Note: sweet, yellow, miniature Korean watermelons from Aloun Farms on O'ahu make a delicious alternative to regular watermelon.)

©iStockphoto.com/Irina

Depending on the context in which it is used, *pūpū* can mean shells or beads. However, in precontact times, *pūpū* were also small bits of food served along with kava, the slightly narcotic root Hawaiians chewed both recreationally and during ceremonies.

Today, *pūpū* is the term used to mean "appetizers," but often constitutes an entire meal, as indicated on invitations by the phrase "heavy *pūpū*." For this reason, *pūpū* generally far exceed the cracker-and-cheese, chips-and-dip approach: they're often protein-rich, filling, and wickedly calorie-laden. (Note: servings are given in appetizer-size portions.)

©iStockphoto.com/OlgaliS

Broiled Sushi

½ c. mayonnaise

½ c. sour cream (nonfat is fine)

2 tsp. sriracha (Thai chile sauce) or more, to taste

2 c. crab, real or imitation (surimi), flaked or chopped

2 Tbsp. minced green onions

4 c. hot sushi rice*

Furikake (Japanese condiment usually sprinkled over rice)

Sesame seeds (mixed black and tan is nice)

Nori or Korean seasoned seaweed (laver) sheets

Preheat broiler to medium. In a bowl, combine mayonnaise, sour cream, and sriracha. Stir in crab and green onions. Set aside; if preparing in advance, cover and refrigerate, then bring to room temperature before continuing. Spread hot sushi rice in 9-by-13-inch casserole. Sprinkle even layer of *furikake* over rice, then spread on crab and dynamite sauce. Scatter layer of sesame seeds over top, then top with more *furikake*. Broil until creamy sauce sets and begins to brown a bit.

Serve with seaweed. (Diners plop a tablespoon or so of broiled sushi on seaweed sheet, roll and eat.)

Serves 24

Variation: Instead of crab, use peeled, roughly chopped, lightly cooked shrimp or fresh, minced, or canned tuna.

Making sushi rice: Combine in saucepan ½ cup white or rice vinegar, ¼ cup sugar, and ¾ teaspoon salt. Heat until salt and sugar dissolve. Place 3 cups hot, steamed, short-grain rice in large bowl. Pour vinegar mixture over rice and gently fold with rice paddle or spatula until thoroughly mixed. (Between folds, fan rice to help evaporate moisture; do not stir in a circular motion and do not mash rice kernels.)

No sriracha?
Use Indonesian sambal oelek (or any ground chile sauce you like); or substitute generous splashes of hot pepper sauce, such as Tobasco.

Broiled sushi, versions of which swept through the Islands in the '90s, employs a version of a sauce contemporary sushi chefs call "dynamite"—a creamy blend of Japanese-style mayonnaise (usually Kewpie brand) and other ingredients, most often sour cream and sriracha, the hot-sweet, bright red ground chile-garlic sauce from Thailand, which cuts the fattiness of this rich blend. Although you can eat broiled sushi with a fork or chopsticks, it's best rolled in crispy, salty, palm-size sheets of Korean-style seasoned seaweed (laver).

Kālua Crostini

1 baguette, thinly sliced

2 garlic cloves, peeled and halved

12 oz. *kālua* pork, chicken, or turkey, shredded

2 Tbsp. very finely minced shallots or sweet onions

1 c. (about 4 oz.) Havarti cheese, grated or finely chopped

Half head cabbage, shredded

Minced green onions or chives for garnish

Preheat oven to 400 degrees. Slice baguette, arrange slices on oven rack, and toast 2 to 3 minutes per side, just until golden brown.

Rub one side of each toasted baguette slice with sliced garlic. Place shredded *kālua* in microwave-safe dish with shallots or onions. Microwave on medium heat for 3 minutes. Stir in grated cheese.

Place oven on broil. Top baguette slices with a little shredded cabbage and a mound of *kālua* pork mixture, then garnish with green onions. Broil briefly. Serve piping hot.

Serves 10 to 12

If you have leftover *kālua* meat (see Chapter 8, Portable *Lū'au*), or live where you can buy prepared *kālua*, this is easy and most luxuriant to serve—a hybrid of Hawaiian and Caucasian concepts in which a little goes a long way.

Edamame: Oh, Mommy!

1 Tbsp. soy sauce

1 Tbsp. Chinese chile oil (La-yu brand, if available)

1 Tbsp. hoisin sauce

1 lb. frozen whole soybeans

1 Tbsp. peanut oil

1 Tbsp. minced garlic

In small bowl or measuring cup, whisk together soy sauce, chile oil, and hoisin sauce. Set aside. Prepare soybeans according to package directions. Drain well. In wok or large frying pan with large bowl or platter nearby, heat peanut oil over high heat. Toss in soybeans and garlic and stir-fry 1 to 2 minutes, until soybeans are heated through and garlic is just turning color. (Do not allow garlic to burn.) Transfer soybeans to bowl or platter, drizzle with soy-chile-hoisin mixture and mix well. Serve hot.

Serves 6 to 8

No Chile Oil?
Use sesame oil, a dash of chile pepper, or hot pepper sauce, such as Tabasco.

©iStockphoto.com/powershot

Little known in America just a few years ago, *edamame,* or whole soybeans, have swept the country and are now available in the freezer cases of many grocery stores, especially Asian ones. They are served shell-on and even novices quickly become adept at mouthing the whole pod and, with a few deft nibbles, working the two or three beans out of the shell. Food that's fun! And when the beans are briefly fried and splashed with such potent Asian flavorings as soy sauce or chile oil, they are elevated to the status of *really* fun food.

Sumiso Seafood Appetizer

1 c. miso (fermented soy paste)

¼ c. soy sauce

¼ c. rice vinegar

¼ c. fresh lemon juice

½ c. sugar

2 Tbsp. Dijon mustard (fine or whole-grain)

2 lb. cooked seafood in bite-size pieces

Pepper

Grated cabbage or whole watercress leaves

In bowl, whisk together miso, soy sauce, vinegar, lemon juice, sugar, and mustard. Set aside. Season seafood with pepper, to taste. Prepare (see below). Line platter or serving plate with cabbage or watercress, add prepared seafood, and drizzle with a little miso sauce.

Provide toothpicks for serving and place bowl of miso sauce alongside for dipping.

Serves 8 to 10

Sumiso is a salty-sweet Japanese sauce or marinade that pairs well with seafood. Use any kind of seafood you like—see suggestions for preparation below.

Seafood options/preparations:

Shrimp: poach whole, peeled shrimp or sauté in a little olive oil and butter.

Scallops: pan-roast scallops in olive oil and butter.

Cuttlefish or squid: clean, score in criss-cross pattern, cut into rings or bite-size pieces, then boil 5 minutes.

Firm-textured white fish: grill or broil swordfish, shark, etc., then cut into bite-size chunks.

Clams: drain canned clams or steam and shell fresh clams.

Ahi: flash-fry seasoned chunks.

©iStockphoto.com/4x6

Bolinhos de Bacalhau/Codfish Croquettes Portuguese-style

1 lb. salt cod, soaked overnight in cold water, well drained

2 russet potatoes, peeled and roughly chopped

Olive oil

½ onion, minced

2-3 cloves garlic, minced

½ c. minced parsley

Paprika

Pepper

2 eggs, beaten

Vegetable oil

Piri-piri Sauce*

> These addictive little poppers are, without question, Portugal's most popular *pūpū*, small plate, or tapas. Once a fixture in Island Portuguese kitchens, you'll be surprised at how irresistible they are—even if you don't care for fish!
>
> (Note: Salt cod is generally sold in two forms: that from Newfoundland, often found in wooden boxes in the seafood chill case; and a harder, dried form, often found in Asian, especially Korean, groceries. The two products are quite different. The Newfoundland type is softer textured, less salty, and, generally, both skinless and boneless, so there's little less waste. If you use the Asian type, allow for loss from bones, skin, and dried bits.)

Place drained cod in saucepan, cover with water, bring to a boil, then turn off heat. Drain and flake cod, removing any bones or skin. Set aside in a medium bowl.

Place potatoes in a saucepan, cover with water, and bring to a boil. Simmer 15 to 20 minutes or until potatoes are tender. Drain. Add to bowl with cod. Drizzle olive oil in sauté pan. Sauté onion, garlic, and parsley over medium-high heat until onion is softened and translucent and parsley is wilted. Add to bowl with cod. Sprinkle with paprika and pepper to taste.

Beat eggs into cod mixture until light and fluffy. Chill, covered, up to 24 hours. With wet hands, roll cod mixture to form golf ball-size spheres, then flatten into thickish cakes . In heavy frying pan or Dutch oven, heat ½-inch depth of vegetable oil over high heat. Simmer at 350 to 360 degrees. With slotted spoon, lower 6 or so croquettes into hot oil. Deep-fry, turning occasionally, until golden-brown and cooked through. To avoid burning, regulate heat as needed. Do not crowd. Add additional oil as needed.

In Portugal, these are routinely served at room temperature. However, if you wish to serve hot, place atop paper towels in heatproof dish and keep warm in oven. For a bit of spice, serve with piri-piri (Portuguese hot sauce)* for dipping.

Serves 6 to 8

* See Piri-piri Sauce p. 79.

Char Siu Bao/ Easy-Steamed Dumplings

1 tsp. vegetable oil

1 c. finely chopped char siu (red roast pork)

2 Tbsp. minced Chinese garlic chives or green onions

2 Tbsp. soy sauce

2 Tbsp. hoisin sauce

2 Tbsp. oyster sauce

1 (1 lb.) loaf frozen, white bread dough, defrosted

   (Bridgford Ready-Dough or Parker House Rolls, if available)

In frying pan, heat vegetable oil over medium-high heat. Add char siu; stir-fry with chives or green onions, soy sauce, hoisin sauce, and oyster sauce for 2 to 3 minutes. Set aside.

Cut loaf-shaped roll of dough into 12 portions. With oiled hands, roll into rounds and flatten. Fill each round with a tablespoon of char siu filling. Pull edges on top of bao, crimping to close. Place each bao on square of waxed paper or kitchen parchment; place in steamer rack. Cover with damp towel; allow to rise 20 to 30 minutes.

Place steamer over simmering water; steam 20 minutes. Dough will spring back when pressed with finger. Serve hot or at room temperature.

Serves 6 (2 buns each)

No char siu? Use the recipe for Nibuta, found on p. 71, or any readily available sweet sausage.

Variation: Cut Chinese sausage (*lup cheong*) into 1 ½-inch lengths; stuff bread rounds with sausage instead of char siu.

Steamed buns or dumplings are a great Hawai'i favorite. They are know to the Chinese as bao ("bow"), and to Islanders as "manapua"—a contraction of the term *mea 'ono pua'a*, which means "delicious pig thing" because the buns are generally stuffed with Chinese roast pork or pork sausage. In the old days, "manapua men" walked the streets with wheeled carts, calling out to prospective customers. Today, Islanders buy bakery boxes full of these buns, each marked with a different food-coloring pattern on top to indicate the nature of the filling. The most common is char siu, sweet roast pork tinged with red food coloring and flavored with Chinese five-spice. Thus the name char siu bao.

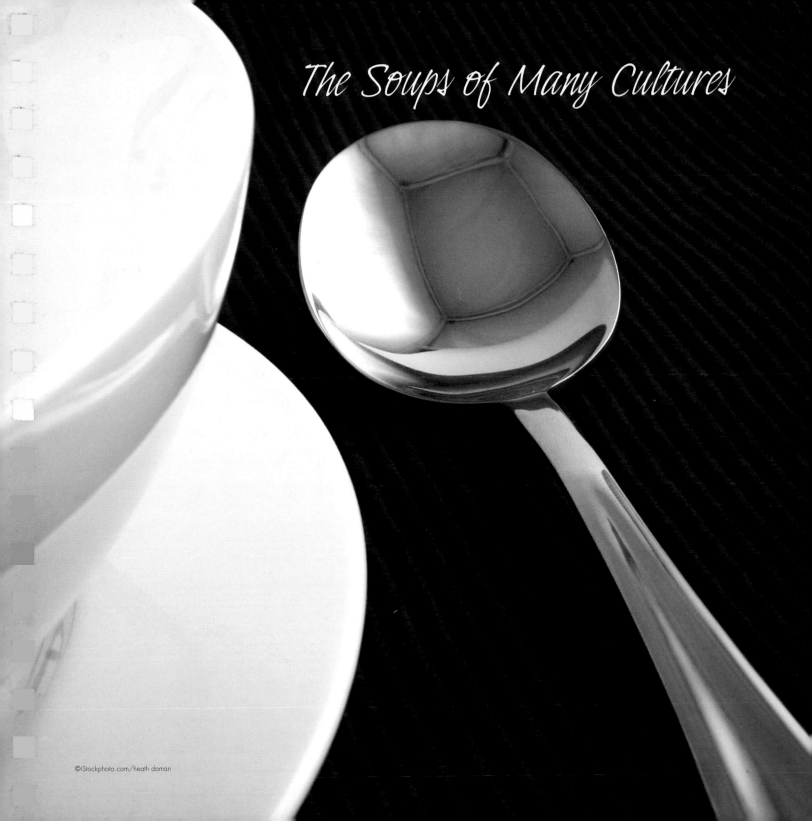

The Soups of Many Cultures

*Y*ou'd think a place as warm as Hawai'i would be a bit down on soups. But virtually all immigrant cultures had soup at the center of their diets and shared their favorites with each other.

Saimin, the Island version of Japanese ramen noodle soup, is practically the state food; it's arguably the most popular late-night snack of the hungry, tired, and broke. Older Portuguese people will tell you that as children they ate soup every day, usually tomato-based with a little meat and lots of vegetables from the family garden. Plus, everyone looks forward to the day after Thanksgiving when, whether you are Chinese or not, you make *jook*, a rice soup with stock made from the turkey carcass. Miso soup, another Island staple, automatically comes with a meal in every local-style Japanese restaurant.

Of course, soups are popular here for the same reasons they are popular everywhere else: they can be inexpensive, easy to "stretch" for large families, and make good use of leftovers. Soups also can be left to simmer on a stove while other work is being done or left for family members when they can't all eat together.

Here's a selection, from sophisticated to homey, and from an array of cultural backgrounds.

©iStockphoto.com/Kelly Cline

Jook/Chinese Rice Soup

6 bone-in chicken thighs

6 c. water

4 cloves garlic, peeled and smashed

2-inch piece ginger, peeled and smashed, divided

1 star anise

2 c. long-grain white rice

8 c. water

1 Tbsp. salt

2 Tbsp. soy sauce

Few drops sesame oil

1/8 tsp. Chinese 5-spice powder

Sesame oil and chopped green onion or Chinese garlic chives for garnish

Place chicken in large saucepan with 6 cups water, garlic, half of the smashed ginger, and star anise. Bring to boil; turn down heat and simmer 30 to 45 minutes, until meat is fully cooked. Remove chicken and shred meat; strain broth. Reserve broth and chicken.

In soup pot, place rice and 8 cups water. Bring to boil; turn heat down and simmer until rice is very soft and falling apart (about 30 minutes). Watch carefully to assure rice doesn't stick.

Drain rice and place in soup pot with chicken broth. Add salt, soy sauce, sesame oil, 5-spice powder, and remaining ginger. If mixture is too thick, add boiling water. Cook over medium to medium-low heat about one hour, until flavors meld and texture is smooth. Return chicken to soup and correct seasonings. Serve garnished with a tiny pool of sesame oil and green onion or chives.

Serves 8

Jook is *not* chicken-rice soup; it's a gruel or porridge almost as thick as oatmeal (and frequently eaten for breakfast). The rice should literally melt, leaving the soup starchy and thick. Made with turkey carcass, this is a favorite post-Thanksgiving soup. This version, however, uses bone-in chicken thighs.

Sinigang Na Baboy/Filipino Sour Pork Soup

1 Tbsp. vegetable oil

1 ½ lb. country-style spare ribs (boneless or almost boneless)

4 cloves (about 1 Tbsp.) garlic, smashed and minced

1 medium onion, peeled and sliced

3 c. water (or tamarind water)

1 c. broth (chicken or pork)

1 c. chopped fresh tomatoes

1 thick slice of tamarind paste (place paste in cloth
    tea bag infuser or pouch made of cheesecloth) or
    1 pkg. *pangsinigang sa sampalok* (tamarind soup mix)

2-inch piece fresh ginger, peeled and smashed

2 bay leaves

1 tsp. ground black pepper

1 tsp. salt

2 tsp. sugar

1 small daikon (Japanese white radish)

½ tsp. Hawaiian or kosher salt

½ lb. green beans, washed and tips trimmed

½ lb. fresh spinach, washed

1 c. edamame (soybeans)

In heavy Dutch oven or soup pot, heat vegetable oil over medium-high heat. Cut spare ribs into 1-inch squares, trimming away any bones. Place pork pieces and bones in oil; fry until golden. Add garlic and onion; cook until onion is golden, wilted, and translucent. Add water, broth, tomatoes, tamarind paste or tamarind soup mix, ginger, bay leaves, pepper, salt, and sugar. Bring to a boil, skimming foam. Simmer 20 to 30 minutes.

Peel daikon, slice into coins, and scatter salt over top. Marinate 10 to 15 minutes, then place in colander and rinse with cold running water. Squeeze dry.

The first time I tasted sinigang, a Filipino-style tamarind soup, I fell in love with the lively flavor of the clear, fresh tasting broth. There are dozens of variations of this piquant soup made with beef, pork, chicken, shrimp (or other seafood), and various vegetables. This one is rather Westernized, using familiar green beans and tomatoes. It is more like a hearty stew, and you can substitute Filipino favorites such as *ampalaya* (bittermelon), ung choy (Chinese water spinach), *otong* (long beans), and *sequa* (sponge gourd). Bok choy, a Chinese cabbage, is a common addition, as is watercress. Don't let the length of the ingredient list put you off—the end result is well worth the effort!

Taste broth and correct seasonings; soup can be held until shortly before serving. Ten or 15 minutes before serving, bring to a boil, then add daikon, green beans, spinach, and edamame. Reduce heat and simmer 10 to 15 minutes, until vegetables are tender. Remove bay leaves and tamarind slice before serving.

Serves 6

Tamarind: *a must-have for this recipe.* Tamarind, the brown, bulbous, acidic pod of the Tamarindus indica tree, helps create the perky flavors found in English Fruity Sauce and Worcestershire sauce, and it is essential to this recipe. You'll find it in Filipino, Asian, and Mexican markets in three forms: fresh pods, peeled pods in cakes or blocks, and as powdered soup mix. To use:

• Fresh pods: immerse a pound or so in water and bring to a boil. Strain and use in place of water or broth in the recipe.

• Tamarind paste: cut a thick slice and place in a cloth tea bag or cheesecloth pouch. (I like to use both tamarind water and tamarind paste.)

• Prepared tamarind soup mix—*pangsinigang sa sampalok* (Tagalog) or *bot me canh chua* (Vietnamese): the least desirable form because it's salty and thin compared to the real thing.

(Note: to find online, just plug "buy tamarind paste" into an online search engine.)

Cold Mango Soup

3 c. fresh mango, peeled, seeded, chopped

2 Tbsp. crystallized ginger, coarsely chopped

1 c. Riesling or Gewürztraminer wine

2 Tbsp. lime juice

1 c. orange juice

1 c. sour cream or crème fraîche

Maple syrup

Fresh mint, snipped or minced, for garnish

No mango?
Use fresh or canned peaches.

Place mango in blender with ginger; puree. Add wine, lime juice, orange juice, and sour cream or crème fraîche. Blend until smooth. Add maple syrup, as needed, for sweetness. Chill until very cold. Serve in decorative glasses or dessert glasses, garnished with mint.

Serves 4 to 6

Cold fruit soup is always an impressive opening for a special summer dinner or as the centerpiece of a warm weather luncheon. Sweet and silky textured mangoes, abundant in late summer, provide a marvelous background for a slightly tangy and tart soup flavored with ginger, wine, lime, and sour cream. Follow this contemporary soup with a mesclun salad topped with a round of warm, nut-crusted goat cheese, or an entrée of poached or grilled fish.

Cozido Made Easy

1 Tbsp. drippings (bacon fat) or butter

2 rings Portuguese sausage (mild or hot), pricked with a fork

2-4 cloves garlic, smashed

Water or chicken broth

6-8 small whole russet, red, or yellow potatoes, peeled

4 carrots, peeled, cut into large chunks

1 bunch kale or collard greens, julienned

½ bunch flat-leaf parsley, minced

Salt and pepper

No linguica?
Use chorizo or kielbasa.

Preheat oven to 325 degrees. In a Dutch oven or large, heavy skillet with heatproof cover, melt drippings and sauté sausages and garlic over medium heat, just until garlic is golden (not burned). Arrange potatoes and carrots around sausage. Pour over enough water or broth just to cover. Bring to a boil, cover, and place in oven. Cook 20 to 25 minutes, until carrots and potatoes are tender when pierced with fork. Scatter kale or collards and parsley on top. Add salt and pepper as desired. Cook another 5 to 10 minutes, until greens are wilted but still bright green. With tongs, remove sausage. Cut roughly into chunks and place in shallow bowls; spoon liquid and vegetables over sausage. Serve with country-style crusty bread.

Serves 6 to 8

Variations: Add a can of diced tomatoes and/or a sliced onion with the potatoes and carrots.

The Portuguese boiled dinner called *cozido* is both a soup and a meaty entrée with several kinds of meats, vegetables, and potatoes simmered together. After cooking for most of the day, *cozido* is separated before being served: the broth is served first (sometimes with the addition of beans, rice, or chickpeas), followed by the tender meat and vegetables. In Hawai'i, the Portuguese enjoy a much quicker boiled dinner (really a braised dinner) with Portuguese sausage (garlicky linguica), cabbage, and potatoes.

Gingery Shrimp Dumpling Soup

For shrimp dumplings:

1 lb. raw peeled and deveined shrimp

1 (8 oz.) can water chestnuts, drained

2 tsp. finely grated ginger

1 Tbsp. soy sauce

1 Tbsp. cornstarch

1 tsp. finely minced Chinese garlic chives or green onion

No watercress?
Use any tender green vegetable: whole leaves of baby spinach, julienned baby bok choy, the sliced leaves and thinly cut stems of Chinese broccoli (*gai lan*, a kale-like vegetable), whole sugar snap peas, or even freshly shelled English peas. Swirl into the hot broth just long enough to cook.

Rinse shrimp in cold water; pat dry with a towel. Finely chop shrimp or pulse in food processor; place in bowl. Rinse water chestnuts in cold running water; drain; pat dry; then mince. Add to shrimp along with grated ginger, soy sauce, and cornstarch. Stir to combine, working mixture well. Cover and chill.

For the soup:

6 c. chicken or pork stock (see recipe p. 50)

Salt, pepper, soy sauce to taste

2 c. tender watercress tops and leaves, cut in 1-inch lengths (discard fibrous ends)

2 stalks Chinese garlic chives or green onion, minced

This "clean-tasting" soup depends entirely on the quality of the broth in which the shrimp and fresh watercress are cooked. Take the time to make a good, rich broth, or use a high quality store-bought broth doctored up with a little ginger (the freshest, least fibrous you can find) and orange peel.

Bring chicken or pork broth to a boil; then reduce heat to a simmer. Add salt and pepper to taste; and splash of soy sauce, if needed.

Form shrimp balls using two dinner spoons, picking up the round ball in one and pushing it into the simmering broth with the other. Add watercress and chives or green onion to broth; cook just until shrimp balls rise to surface and watercress is bright green (about one minute). Serve immediately.

Serves 4 to 6

Chinese-style Soup Stock

Place 3 pounds bone-in chicken or bone-in pork in 12 cups water. Bring to a boil, skimming foam. Add 2-inch piece of peeled, smashed, sliced fresh ginger; 1 whole star anise, 1 teaspoon dried orange or tangerine peel, and 5 dried shiitake mushrooms. Simmer 1 to 2 hours. Strain through cheesecloth or muslin; meat may be removed from bone, added to soup, or used as desired.

Makes about 10 cups delicately flavored stock.

Grating Ginger

The best way to grate ginger is with a Japanese-style porcelain grater, called a *shoga oroshi*, which is especially designed for this purpose. Peeled ginger is rubbed in a circular motion over a grating surface that is comprised of needle-sharp points. A surrounding indentation acts like a moat to capture the ginger juice. If you don't have one of these graters, use a fine Microplane rasp or the finest holes of a conventional grater.

Crab Miso Soup

4 c. dashi (Japanese fish stock)*

Splash of sake or sherry

2 tsp. lemon, lime, or yuzu (Japanese citrus) juice

2 tsp. soy sauce

6-8 oz. steamed fresh crab, cracked and cleaned, preferably still warm**

3 Tbsp. white miso (fermented soy paste)

1 stalk green onion, white and green parts, minced

Bring dashi to a boil, then reduce to a simmer. Add sake or sherry, citrus, and soy sauce. Allow flavors to meld for a few minutes. Correct seasonings. Divide warm crab among each of four deep, Japanese-style bowls, preferably with lids. Pour broth over crab. Place miso in a small strainer and use the back of a spoon or pestle to push equal parts miso into each bowl. Swirl with a chopstick to mix. Garnish with green onion. Serve immediately.

Serves 4

*Read more about dashi on p. 89, Sides chapter.

**Any form of cooked crab or even imitation crab (surimi) may be used, but fresh-steamed is best.

Miso soup has as many variations as there are Japanese households and days of the year. The basic formula is pristine: dashi (Japanese fish stock), miso with a little soy sauce for flavor, tiny squares of tofu, and green onion as garnish floating in the broth. This decadent version makes a great starter for a special meal.

©iStockphoto.com/Sharon Kennedy

Salads

The Island Way

*I*sland salads are no ordinary lettuce-tomato-cucumber mixtures. We go for the gusto with a variety of ingredients and tastes. Experiment with the offerings here—you'll give your guests a tantalizing treat and surely find some new, can't-live-without-them favorites.

Warm Shiitake Salad

3 Tbsp. soy sauce

1 ½ Tbsp. lemon juice

1 ½ Tbsp. lime juice

1 tsp. mirin (Japanese sweet cooking seasoning)

1 tsp. rice vinegar

½ lb. fresh shiitake mushrooms

Nonstick spray

1 shallot, thinly sliced

2 Tbsp. butter

Salt and freshly ground pepper

Shredded cabbage

No shiitake? Use any fresh meaty mushroom.

In small bowl, combine soy sauce, lemon and lime juices, mirin, and rice vinegar. Set aside. Clean mushrooms with damp paper towel. Slice mushrooms thinly. Heat nonstick pan over medium-high heat; spray with nonstick spray. Lay shiitake slices flat in pan and scatter shallots over. Cook over medium-high heat for 5 minutes. Add butter, reduce heat to low and cook another 5 minutes, stirring and flipping mushrooms until they are well browned and have lost most of their moisture. Season with salt and freshly ground pepper, drizzle with soy-citrus dressing. Serve warm on a bed of shredded cabbage.

Serves 4

More a side dish than a salad, this recipe comes together quickly. Make the dressing and slice the mushrooms in advance, then cook the mushrooms just before serving.

The Gilded Avocado

2 firm-ripe avocados, chilled

Juice of 2 lemons

2-3 Tbsp. tobiko or other roe or caviar

Soy sauce

Chill four salad plates. On a cutting board, peel, seed, and thinly slice avocado, being careful not to mash or bruise the fruit. Drizzle lemon juice over avocado to prevent oxidation. Divide slices between salad plates, fanning attractively. Scatter tobiko or other roe or caviar over avocado. Serve, passing soy sauce for those who wish to drizzle it over the dish.

Serves 4

No tobiko?
Use the best caviar
you can afford.

This pristine dish is the perfect combination of silk and crunch: creamy firm-ripe avocado slices topped with tiny crimson spheres of crisp-juicy, salty-sweet fish eggs. It's an ideal salad to serve when you wish to impress friends. Tobiko (flying fish roe) comes in a variety of flavors and colors; orange, used in this recipe, is the natural color.

Tofu-Watercress Salad with Asian-Style Dressing

For the salad:

1 (14 oz.) block firm tofu

1 bunch watercress

1 c. mung bean sprouts

1 small sweet onion, sliced very thin

2 medium ripe tomatoes, cut into small chunks

1 (6 oz.) can chunk tuna, drained (optional)

Drain tofu, place on a flat plate and place another flat plate on top; weight with canned goods or by other means and press out liquid for 30 minutes or so. Drain liquid; cut tofu into small squares. Place on paper towels in a microwave-safe dish, then microwave on high for 4 minutes. Drain off any additional water and place on fresh paper towels.

Bring large pot of water to boil; plunge watercress into water. As soon as water returns to a boil, transfer watercress to colander and run underneath cold water. Press or wring out excess moisture. Cut into 2-inch lengths and place in large salad bowl. Blanch bean sprouts in similar manner. Add to watercress, along with onions, tomatoes, and tuna (if using). Add drained tofu; gently toss. Cover with plastic wrap; refrigerate until cold.

For the dressing:

2 tsp. sesame oil

2 cloves garlic, pressed through a garlic press

6 Tbsp. soy sauce

1 ½ tsp. sugar

1 Tbsp. brown sugar

2 Tbsp. mirin (Japanese sweet cooking seasoning)

1 Tbsp. miso (fermented soy paste)

2 tsp. rice vinegar

In small saucepan, gently heat sesame oil and add garlic, heating just until garlic sizzles; remove from heat, strain; discard garlic. Combine garlic-flavored sesame oil with soy sauce, sugars, mirin, miso, and rice vinegar. Whisk together. Dress salad just before serving.

Serves 6 to 8

Protein- and fiber-rich, and refreshingly crunchy, tofu-watercress salad is both a deli and a potluck staple. It can be as simple as chunks of tofu, blanched watercress, and sliced tomato adorned with a garlicky dressing of oil and soy sauce, yet there are dozens of variations. Islanders often incorporate canned tuna, but canned or poached fresh salmon is another option.

A word about watercress: Island watercress is a hardy, leggy, long-stemmed plant that is almost always blanched before use. Watercress is a year-round staple in Island stores but is less readily available elsewhere in the United States. When it is available, mainland watercress is a delicate creature: short-stemmed and leafier. Chop and use it fresh, without blanching. Any crunchy green vegetable can be substituted in tofu salad; try fresh arugula or frisée, blanched bok choy, or French-sliced blanched green beans.

Pickled Cucumber Salad

1 lb. fresh cucumber (2 regular cucumbers or 1 long English cucumber)

Pinch or two Hawaiian or kosher salt

2 Tbsp. rice vinegar or distilled white vinegar

3 Tbsp. brown sugar

2 Tbsp. ginger, peeled and finely sliced

Peel cucumber, leaving thin strips of green. Slice thinly, place in bowl, scatter salt over top. Set aside for 10 to 15 minutes while cucumber releases its water. Place cucumber in colander; rinse off salt with cold running water; wrap in paper towels and press out excess water. Place in container with lid. In small bowl or measuring cup, mix together vinegar, brown sugar, and ginger; pour over cucumber. Marinate in refrigerator 1 hour; drain; remove ginger. Correct seasonings.

Serves 4

This fresh sweet-sour pickle goes well with fish dishes. It's powerfully flavored, so small servings are customary.

Usunuba Usachi/Okinawan Chard and Tofu Salad

1 bunch Swiss chard

10 oz. tofu (may be silken or firm type)

2 Tbsp. tahini (sesame butter)

2 Tbsp. miso (fermented soy paste)

1 Tbsp. sugar

1 Tbsp. soy sauce

2 Tbsp. sesame seeds, toasted and ground

©iStockphoto.com/Charlotte Moss

Wash chard well in cold running water. Place individual leaves on cutting board and make v-shaped cut to release stem from leaf. Cut stems in 1/2-inch pieces. Bring large pot of water to full, rolling boil. Drop in stems; cook 2 minutes. Add leaves; cook 2 minutes more. Drain well and bathe in cold water to stop cooking. Wrap in three or four layers of paper towels, then squeeze and press to remove as much liquid as possible. Chop roughly and refrigerate.

Bring medium-size saucepan of water to boil. Cut tofu into slices or chunks; drop into boiling water; boil 2 minutes. Drain well in colander. Place tofu in a suribachi (a grooved Japanese mortar and pestle), if you have one, along with tahini, miso, sugar, and soy sauce; grind into a paste. Otherwise, use back of wooden spoon and mix well. Combine tofu sauce with chard. Correct seasonings. Refrigerate in airtight container. Serve within 24 hours, garnished with sesame seeds.

Serves 4

Shira ae, a Japanese salad made with a light tofu dressing, is one of my favorites. It's refreshing, especially in warm weather; convenient, because you can make it ahead of time; and healthful, being low in saturated fats and offering all the nutritional benefits of tofu (protein, minerals, antioxidants) and dark, leafy greens (vitamins A, B, and C, beta-carotene, fiber, calcium, and carotenoids). This is the Okinawan version of *shira ae*, enlivened by a touch of sesame.

Ensaladang Labag/Radish and Orange Salad

1 small daikon radish (about 8 oz.) or equivalent red radishes

¼ tsp. rock salt

1 c. fresh orange or tangerine slices, seeded

¼ tsp. salt

Juice of 1 lemon

1 tsp. patis (fish sauce, optional)

Shredded cabbage and cilantro sprigs for garnish

Peel daikon/radishes; slice into small rounds or half-moons. Place in glass dish, scatter rock salt over top, and marinate for 20 minutes. Place radishes in colander; rinse well with cold water. Press out water.

In medium bowl, combine daikon/radishes, orange or tangerine slices, salt, lemon, and fish sauce, if using. Chill. Serve on bed of shredded cabbage with sprig of cilantro, if desired.

Serves 2 to 4

Variations: Substitute tomatoes for oranges or tangerines. Add sweet onion slices.

> This salad from the Philippines combines the joy of crunchiness with the sweetness of citrus. A splash of fish sauce adds a sophisticated brininess.

Vietnamese Carrot Salad

2 cucumbers, peeled, seeded, and julienned

3 carrots, peeled and julienned

1 stalk celery, finely sliced

1 small green bell pepper, seeded and julienned

1 (1-inch) piece of ginger, peeled and finely grated

For dressing:

¼ c. vegetable oil

¼ c. rice vinegar

1 tsp. sugar

1 tsp. lemon or lime juice

1 tsp. fish sauce (optional)

A few drops sesame oil

Salt and pepper, to taste

For garnish:

½ c. roasted peanuts, chopped

This salad is all about texture—the finely grated ingredients, the silkiness of the dressing, and the crunch of the peanuts. To save time and effort, use a food processor with the grater blade or a mandoline.

©iStockphoto.com/ranplett

In salad bowl, combine cucumbers, carrots, celery, bell pepper, and ginger. In bowl or cruet, combine dressing ingredients; correct seasonings, as desired. Pour dressing over salad; cover and refrigerate just long enough to chill. Garnish with chopped peanuts.

Serves 4 to 6

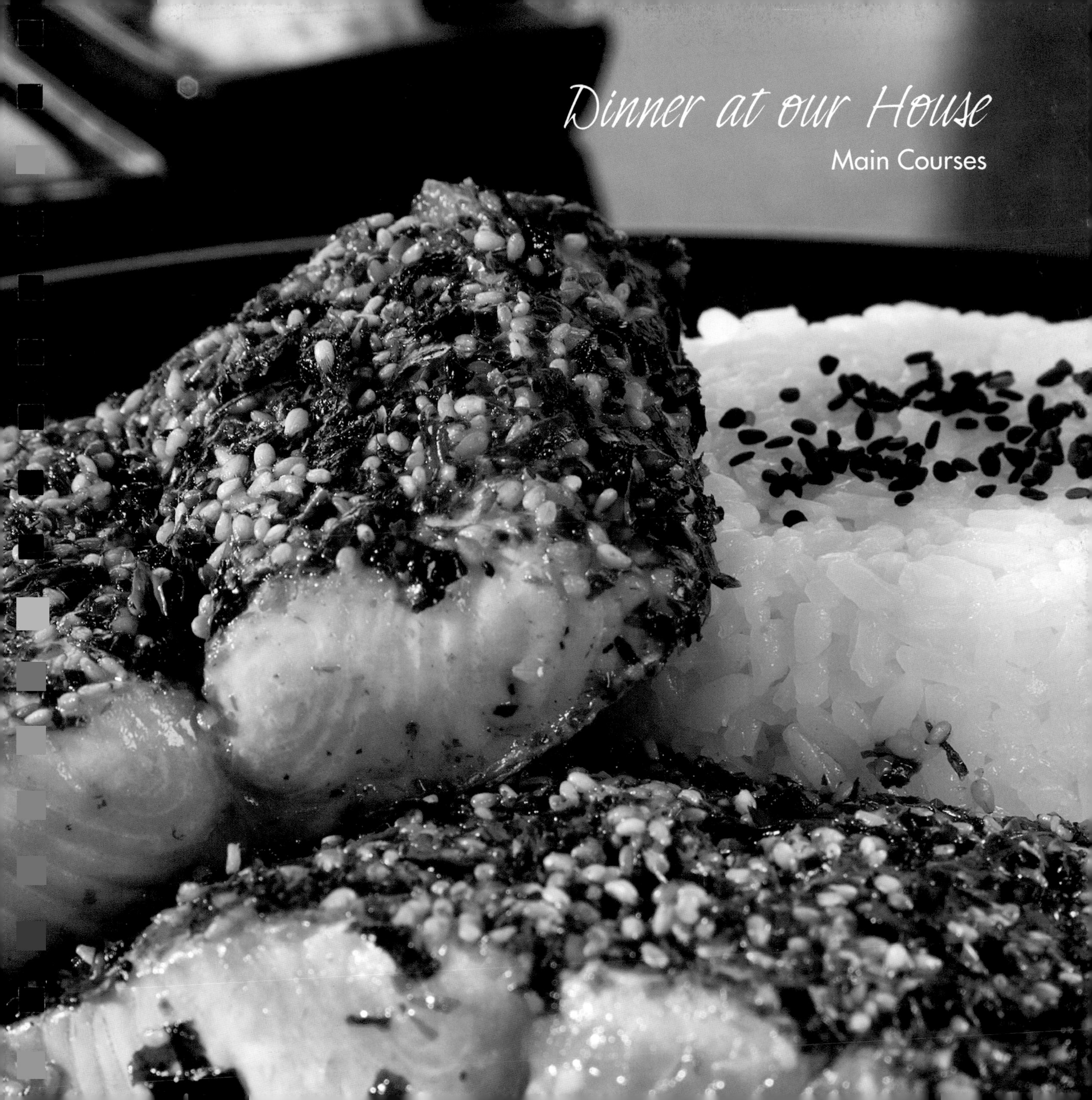
Dinner at our House
Main Courses

*A*lthough Hawai'i is typically informal, we do enjoy dress-up sit-down gatherings from time to time. A dinner with friends at home, whether around a formal dining room table or at a picnic table in the carport, allows for intimate conversation and for showing off our fanciest dishes. These are some of the recipes we choose.

Rafute/Okinawan Shoyu Pork

3-4 lb. pork shoulder, pork butt, pork belly, or other well-marbled boneless pork cut

2 c. pork and/or chicken stock, or mixed dashi (Japanese fish stock) and pork or chicken stock

1 c. Japanese-style soy sauce (Kikkoman or Yamasa are readily available), divided

4-inch piece fresh ginger, peeled and sliced

2 cloves garlic, sliced

1 c. sugar

1 c. awamori, sake, dry sherry, whiskey, or Scotch

½ c. mirin (Japanese sweet cooking seasoning, optional)

Cover pork with water in saucepan. Bring to a boil, skimming foam. Turn down heat, simmer 30 to 40 minutes. Remove pork, reserving stock, cool, then slice into pieces about 2 inches square and ½- to ¾-inch thick.

Place stock in large saucepan, add ½ cup soy sauce, and bring to a boil. Add pork, ginger, and garlic; gently simmer over low heat, covered, for 1 hour. Add the remaining soy sauce, sugar, and awamori or sherry. Cook about 20 minutes until pork is tender. Add mirin; cook an additional 30 minutes.

Pork can be refrigerated, then gently reheated in stock or sake (not water, which robs the meat of its tenderness). Chunks of tofu and sliced vegetables can be heated with meat to stretch this dish.

Serves 12 to 24, depending on whether this rich dish is served as an entrée, in smaller appetizer portions, or stretched by stir-frying with tofu and vegetables.

Rafute, or pork simmered in soy sauce stock, is the national dish of Okinawa. Every cook has a slightly different formula, but the necessary elements are a well-marbled cut of pork, a blend of meat and fish stock, soy sauce, ginger, sugar, and spirits. The dish is cooked in two stages: first the pork is boiled to tenderize it and melt the fat, then it is simmered slowly in a highly flavored sweet sauce. It's quite rich, so just a few small slices are served over hot rice. Or, more typically, the pork is used in the manner of ham or prosciutto to add bits of intense flavor to vegetable stir-fries, rice, noodle dishes, or soups.

Pork Guisantes/Pork and Peas

1 lb. boneless pork butt or other well-marbled pork roast

3-5 cloves garlic, minced

4-8 bay leaves

1 tsp. salt

1 Tbsp. whole peppercorns, crushed (or coarsely ground pepper)

Pinch of red pepper flakes

1 medium onion, thinly sliced

½ c. water

¼ c. tomato paste

1 c. frozen peas

Separate fat from lean meat of pork, slicing lean meat into stir-fry sized strips. Over high heat, in large sauté pan, Dutch oven, or wok, render pork fat until melted (about 2 teaspoons total). Pour out excess fat, scrape up any solids and discard. Reduce heat to medium-high; add pork, garlic, bay leaves, salt, peppers, and onions. Stir-fry 5 to 7 minutes until pork is cooked through. Add water and tomato paste; simmer until liquid is mostly evaporated. Add peas, stirring to break up frozen clumps. Simmer briefly, just until peas are bright green and warmed through. Serve immediately over hot rice.

Serves 4

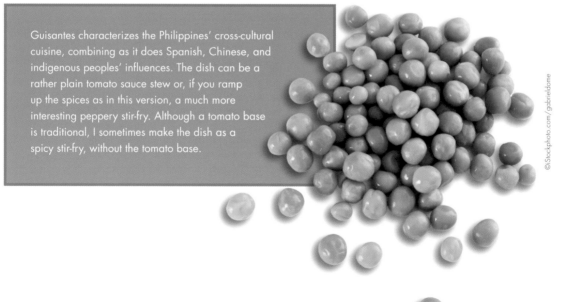

Guisantes characterizes the Philippines' cross-cultural cuisine, combining as it does Spanish, Chinese, and indigenous peoples' influences. The dish can be a rather plain tomato sauce stew or, if you ramp up the spices as in this version, a much more interesting peppery stir-fry. Although a tomato base is traditional, I sometimes make the dish as a spicy stir-fry, without the tomato base.

©iStockphoto.com/gabrieldome

Nibuta/Slow-Simmered Pork

2-3 lb. pork butt roast, trimmed of excess fat

2 cloves garlic, sliced

2-inch piece fresh ginger, peeled and sliced

Vegetable oil

4 c. water

¼ head cabbage, shredded or roughly chopped

1 star anise

½ bunch green onions, sliced

½ c. mirin (Japanese sweet cooking seasoning)

½ c. sake

½ c. shoyu

1 c. sugar

Trim pork butt into two long lengths; truss lengthwise and crosswise with kitchen string to form a neat, rolled packet. Slice garlic and ginger on cutting board; smash by laying blade of Chinese cleaver sideways on top of the garlic and ginger and hitting firmly with fist. In Dutch oven, heat 1 tablespoon vegetable oil over medium-high heat. Brown roast on all sides; drain oil. Add garlic, ginger, water, cabbage, star anise, and green onions; bring to a boil, skimming residue; simmer for 1 hour.

Drain broth from pork; reserve to use for Japanese noodle soup (saimin or ramen). In bowl, combine mirin, sake, shoyu, and sugar; stir until sugar is dissolved. Return pork to pot; pour mirin mixture over top. Bring to boil; reduce heat and simmer for 30 minutes. Remove from heat; allow meat to rest 10 to 15 minutes, then remove it and slice thinly. Serve over hot rice with stir-fried vegetables, or use to garnish Japanese noodle soup (saimin or ramen). If you wish, reduce shoyu mixture until it's thick and syrupy; then, drizzle over pork, hot rice, and vegetables.

Serves 6 to 8, when paired with noodles and/or rice and vegetables

©iStockphoto.com/Thomas Perkins

Nibuta is Japanese pot roast pork, most often served in Hawai'i as a hearty garnish floating atop a bowl of saimin (Japanese-style noodle soup). When served over hot rice or noodles and crunchy, stir-fried vegetables, the roast also makes a fine—and quite rich!—entrée.

Grilled 'Ahi with Soybean Purée

½ lb. frozen shelled edamame (soybeans)

3 Tbsp. butter, divided

2 tsp. soy sauce

1 ½ c. rich chicken broth, divided

½ medium onion, sliced

1 garlic clove, sliced

1 Tbsp. balsamic vinegar

Salt and pepper

2 (3-4 oz.) 'ahi steaks

Boil edamame according to package directions; taste to be sure soybeans are tender, not crunchy. Drain. In food processor fitted with metal blade, purée hot soybeans with 2 tablespoons butter and soy sauce. Scrape down bowl occasionally and drizzle in 1 tablespoon chicken broth until a thin purée consistency is achieved. Place purée in small saucepan, then place that saucepan into larger saucepan of hot water on low heat to keep warm. Melt remaining butter and sauté onion until limp and translucent. Add remaining chicken stock and boil 10 to 15 minutes, until reduced by half. Add garlic and balsamic vinegar; cook a few additional minutes. Strain sauce into a saucepan, boil until reduced by half and somewhat syrupy. Add salt and pepper as desired. Warm two plates in oven. Grill or broil 'ahi until desired doneness (medium-rare is preferred, about 3 to 6 minutes per side). Place a pool of warm soybean purée on each plate, top with 'ahi, drizzle with balsamic sauce.

Serves 2; multiply for as many servings as desired

No soybeans? Use lima or fava beans.

When you serve 'ahi, you're saying the evening is special. Though pricey, 'ahi (bigeye or yellowfin tuna) is easily the favorite fish of most Islanders—our equivalent of steak. In this recipe, steamed soybeans are transformed into an elegant, silky-textured purée to complement the fish. Balsamic vinegar (use the best you can afford) is cooked down to form a beautifully balanced sauce. You can also perk up your guests' taste buds with a spicy wasabi butter.

Variation with Wasabi Butter: Instead of the onion/balsamic sauce, serve the grilled fish with wasabi butter, which is easily prepared in advance. Purée or mash together 3 tablespoons chilled butter and 1 to 3 tablespoons wasabi; place on a length of plastic wrap; roll into a log, twisting to secure each end. Refrigerate.

Crispy Fish with Tomato-Basil Relish

2 c. chopped ripe tomatoes (cherry-type, salad, or heirloom)

½ c. julienned fresh basil

2-4 cloves garlic, minced

¼ c. extra virgin olive oil

1-2 Tbsp. balsamic vinegar

½ tsp. salt

¼ tsp. freshly ground black pepper

Sugar (optional)

4 (3-4 oz.) boneless fillets of white-fleshed fish

Cornstarch

Salt and freshly ground black pepper

Vegetable oil

Combine tomatoes, basil, garlic, olive oil, vinegar, salt, and pepper. Taste and correct seasonings; if tomatoes are very acidic, add a pinch of sugar to balance flavors. Other minced fresh herbs or aromatics (oregano, marjoram, thyme, minced onions, scallions, chives) may be added to vary flavors. Set aside to allow flavors to meld.

Wipe fish with wet paper towels and place on flat plate or cutting board. Using a small strainer filled with cornstarch, dust with cornstarch, turning to coat both sides. Sprinkle generously with salt and pepper. In frying pan, heat ⅛ inch vegetable oil over medium-high heat. Reduce heat to medium, fry fish on both sides until golden brown. Place fillets on warm plates, topping each with a scattering of tomato-basil relish.

Serves 4

This dish came about one day when I had fresh monchong, an exceptionally moist, delicate, white-fleshed fish also known as pomfret, and beautiful grape tomatoes. The relish, minus the fish, is also wonderful atop bruschetta, Italian-style garlic toasts.

Pork Chop Adobo/Filipino-style Pork Chops

Vegetable oil

4 extra-thick pork chops

4 cloves garlic, smashed

½ onion, thinly sliced

2 Tbsp. cider vinegar or Filipino sugarcane vinegar

2 bay leaves, broken in half

1-2 peppercorns

¼ c. soy sauce

Preheat oven to warm (150 degrees). Cover bottom of large sauté pan with ⅛ inch vegetable oil; heat on high. Once oil begins to simmer, sear pork chops, 3 minutes per side. Transfer to heatproof plate, cover with foil tent, and place in warm oven.

Reduce heat to medium-low; gently sauté garlic and onion, cooking until garlic is golden and onion is limp and translucent (do not allow to burn). Add vinegar, bay leaves, peppercorns, and soy sauce. Simmer 10 minutes. Add chops to sauce and cook until done, 5 to 7 minutes (145 degrees internal temperature on an instant-read thermometer). Discard bay leaves and peppercorns, divide pork chops among 4 plates, and drizzle sauce over top.

Serves 4

For this quick, piquant entrée, which is a version of adobo (the national dish of the Philippines), choose the thickest pork chops you can find; thin chops dry out quickly. This makes a wonderful meal with a Filipino-style salad, garlic rice, and savory banana fritters (see garlic rice recipe on p. 90 and banana fritters recipe on p. 94). To make sure the pork doesn't overcook, use an instant-read thermometer.

Furikake Salmon

Mayonnaise

Wasabi

Milk

2 salmon fillets or steaks

Furikake (Japanese condiment usually sprinkled over rice)

Vegetable oil

For each serving, combine 2 tablespoons mayonnaise with a teaspoon or so of wasabi to taste, and thin to sauce texture with a few drops of milk; adjust mayonnaise or wasabi, as desired. Cover and refrigerate.

Wipe fillets or steaks with damp paper towel. Sprinkle layer of *furikake* onto a cutting board or flat plate and coat salmon generously on both sides. In sauté pan, heat ½ inch vegetable oil over medium-high heat until quite hot. Fry salmon 3 to 5 minutes per side, until lightly browned and opaque on surface. Spread half the wasabi mayonnaise on a plate; top with salmon fillet or steak; drizzle some more mayonnaise on top.

Serves 2; multiply for as many servings as desired

Furikake, which became quite the rage in the '90s, is a blend of Japanese seasonings that combine crisp-dried nori with salt, pepper, and other ingredients. It becomes a sort of breading for this pan-fried salmon, dressed with a tasty mayonnaise sauce made with wasabi. Serve with hot rice (with a sprinkle of *furikake* on top), stir-fried vegetables, or a green salad.

No furikake?
Finely chop nori, then combine with toasted sesame seeds and a little salt and pepper. Or just use toasted sesame seeds.

Bulgogi/Korean Barbecued Beef

¼ c. soy sauce

¼ c. lemon juice

3 Tbsp. vegetable oil

1 Tbsp. sesame oil

¼ c. minced onion

1 Tbsp. corn syrup

1 Tbsp. brown sugar

2 Tbsp. sesame seeds, toasted and ground

2 cloves garlic, minced

¼ c. minced green onion (green and white parts)

Pinch of Korean hot red pepper threads (*sil kochu*) or red pepper flakes

½ tsp. salt

2 lb. beef *

Shredded cabbage and toasted pine nuts for garnish

In a large flat container with a cover, combine all ingredients except steak and garnish. Place steak in marinade and massage marinade into steak, turning. Spread steak out. Refrigerate 1 to 3 hours. Grill over hot coals, broil, or pan-grill in ridged cast iron frying pan until steak is cooked through, making sure not to overcook. With sharp knife, cut into bite-size pieces. Serve on bed of shredded cabbage, garnished with toasted pine nuts.

Serves 4

* Cuts of meat to use: Many different cuts can be used for this dish. In Hawai'i, flank steak is common: remove tendon, trim steak, and score in criss-cross pattern across grain. I've used well-marbled, thin-cut chuck steak with success. But in Korea, much more tender cuts are preferred: tenderloin roast, eye of round, and sirloin. The steak must be thinly cut—¼ inch or thereabouts. If you can't find a precut piece that works, have a butcher make the cuts for you.

Korea has two signature barbecued beef dishes: *kal bi* (barbecued short ribs) and *bulgogi*. While the thinly sliced, cross-cut short ribs needed for *kal bi* can be hard to find outside of Hawai'i or Korean neighborhoods, *bulgogi* can be made with any thin-sliced steak or roast. Serve as an entrée, with rice and salad, or as a *pūpū*.

Portuguese-style Salmon with Tomato Gravy

2 tsp. olive oil

2 tsp. butter

1 lb. skinless, boneless salmon fillet, cut into four pieces

1 medium onion, sliced

1 celery stalk, sliced

3 cloves fresh garlic, minced

1-2 small hot red chile peppers, minced (optional)*

½ bunch fresh flat-leaf parsley, chopped

¼ c. red wine vinegar

1 (14 ½ oz.) can diced tomatoes

1 (8 oz.) can tomato sauce

3 potatoes, peeled and sliced

Handful of chopped, seeded green olives

¼ tsp. ground black pepper

Salt to taste

Preheat oven to warm (150 degrees or less). In large sauté pan or wok, heat olive oil and butter over medium-high heat, then sear salmon briefly. Remove from pan, place in heatproof dish, cover with foil tent, and reserve in warm oven. Sauté onion, celery, garlic, peppers, and parsley in remaining oil and butter until wilted and translucent. Add vinegar, tomatoes, tomato sauce, then arrange potatoes in pan. Simmer over medium heat until potatoes are tender. Return salmon to sauce, add olives and season with salt and pepper, heat through and serve.

Serves 4

* *Variation using piri-piri sauce:* Instead of chiles, let everyone add their own heat to the dish by passing piri-piri, the standard Portuguese hot sauce. To make a simple piri-piri (there are hundreds of variations), combine ¼ cup minced fresh, hot peppers (such as small red Hawaiian peppers or Thai chiles) with 3 cloves minced garlic, a generous pinch of salt, and 1 cup olive oil. Store in airtight jar in refrigerator. A splash of lemon juice or vinegar is often added to further heighten the flavor.

In the homey old days, tomato gravy with canned salmon or mackerel was a favorite weeknight supper. This contemporary version employs fresh salmon fillets and is dressed up with chiles and olives. Tradition is to serve this dish over potatoes. As in this recipe, the potatoes can cook right in the sauce. Or skip that step and serve fish over garlic mashed potatoes.

Chinese-style Steamed Fish

1 (2-3 lb.) whole fish or equivalent steaks or thick fillets

2 Tbsp. plus 1 tsp. sesame oil

2 Tbsp. minced or grated ginger

Salt and pepper to taste

¼ c. peanut oil

3 stalks green onion or chives, green part only, minced

2 Tbsp. soy sauce

Shredded cabbage and sprigs of cilantro for garnish

Drizzle fish with 2 tablespoons sesame oil and sprinkle with 1 tablespoon ginger and generous amount of salt and pepper. Marinate 1 hour.

Steam fish (see technique below). Meanwhile, in small saucepan, heat peanut oil and remaining sesame oil over medium-high heat until sizzling.

Place bed of shredded cabbage on plate or platter. Arrange cooked fish atop cabbage. Dress fish with remaining ginger, green onion or chives, and sprigs of cilantro; top with sizzling oil and drizzle of soy sauce. Serve immediately.

Serves 2 to 4, depending on appetite and accompanying dishes

To prepare whole fish for steaming: slit down center of belly and remove innards from stomach cavity. Rinse in cold, running water; pat dry. To aid in cooking, use very sharp knife to score loin on both sides in criss-cross pattern. Head and gills may be removed or not, as desired.

Easy steaming: place a couple of inches of water in the bottom of a wok, bring to a boil, then turn down to medium heat. Place fish on a round rack, place rack over simmering water, and cover wok. Steam until fish is opaque and just beginning to flake.

This beloved dish, in which steamed fish is drizzled with sizzling peanut and sesame oils and a bit of soy sauce, is a Chinese standard. Whole fish is most commonly used, but thick steaks or whole sides can be substituted if timing is carefully attended to. Favorite fish for this are mullet, *moi, akule,* and *kūmū,* but you may use any mild-flavored white fish and even trout, bass, or catfish. For parties, choose carefree, make-ahead side dishes, or recruit help since the cook will be busy with the fish until the very last minute.

Fish Baked in Coconut Milk

4 (4-6 oz.) fillets of white-fleshed fish

¼ c. lemon, lime, calamansi, or Hawaiian lime juice

Salt and pepper

2-inch piece fresh ginger, peeled, sliced, and smashed

5-inch length lemongrass

3-4 kaffir lime leaves

2-3 cloves garlic, peeled, smashed

1 (14 ½ oz.) can coconut milk or equivalent fresh coconut milk

Several sprigs of cilantro (also called Chinese parsley or coriander)

Preheat oven to 350 degrees. In heatproof casserole, sprinkle fish fillets with citrus juice and dust with salt and pepper. Scatter ginger, lemongrass, kaffir lime leaves, and garlic over fish. Pour coconut milk over top, cover, and place in oven. Bake about 20 minutes, until fish is cooked through. Garnish with cilantro.

Serves 4

No kaffir lime leaves or lemongrass? That's OK; this dish is fine without them.

Fish baked or simmered in coconut milk is found throughout Asia and the Pacific. This version combines elements of dishes from the Philippines and Southeast Asia. It's best with white-fleshed, mild-flavored fish—anything from moonfish to halibut or snapper to *mahimahi*. If you can find calamansi, the miniature limes of the Philippines, use them—they are both piquant and flavorful, like a marriage of orange and lime.

Izakaya Karaage Oyako/Japanese Tavern-style Fried Chicken

8 skin-on boneless chicken thighs

4 Tbsp. soy sauce

4 Tbsp. mirin (Japanese sweet cooking seasoning)

4 Tbsp. sake

2 tsp. (about 3 cloves) minced garlic

1 tsp. shichimi togarashi or 7-spice powder, (optional)

Pinch of salt

Cornstarch

Panko (Japanese-style bread crumbs)

Oil for frying

Lemon wedges and minced green onion for garnish

Rinse chicken in cold water and pat dry. Place in 9-by-13-inch glass dish. In a 2-cup measure, combine soy sauce, mirin, sake, garlic, togarashi, and salt. Pour over chicken; marinate 30 minutes. Preheat oven to 150-200 degrees. Line heatproof dish with paper towels. In large, heavy frying pan or Dutch oven, heat 1 to 2 inches of oil to 375 degrees for about 10 minutes. (Check temperature with deep-frying thermometer, or note these signs: oil will shimmer, and a cube of bread dropped into the oil will brown in a minute or so.)

Izakaya, or Japanese taverns, have proliferated in the Islands in recent years, with menus focused on small plates that pair well with beer and sake. Among the dishes often encountered in these establishments is chicken karaage, marinated deep-fried chicken.

While oil heats, prepare for frying in assembly line fashion: place cornstarch in small, hand-held strainer and sift onto flat plate or square of waxed paper, place panko on a flat plate or square of waxed paper. When oil is heated, use tongs to remove chicken from marinade and shake to remove excess moisture. Roll first in cornstarch and then in panko; use two forks to avoid caking your fingers with breading. Deep-fry two or three pieces of chicken at a time so they aren't crowded and oil remains at correct temperature, for 4 to 5 minutes, until golden-brown and cooked through. Place on towel-lined dish in warmed oven until all the chicken is fried. Just before serving, drizzle lemon juice over chicken and scatter minced green onions over top; serve with hot steamed rice.

Serves 4 to 6

On the Side

Potatoes, Rice, and More

*T*hey may be on the side but that doesn't mean we don't care about them: mac salad, potato and rice dishes, and ethnic vegetable dishes of all kinds are integral to our plate lunch culture. A whole book could be written on sides alone. Here are just a few that we enjoy.

Curried Sweet Potato Salad

2 lb. cooked, peeled sweet potatoes

½ c. thinly sliced celery

½ c. diced Maui or other sweet onion

½ c. raisins

¼ c. plain yogurt (nonfat, low-fat, regular)

2 Tbsp. mayonnaise (regular or reduced-fat)

2-4 Tbsp. mango chutney

1 Tbsp. orange juice concentrate

1-2 tsp. curry powder (to taste)

½ tsp. ground cumin

Salt and pepper to taste

½ c. coarsely chopped toasted nuts (almonds, pecans, walnuts, or macadamias)

Greens (optional, used as base for salad)

Cut cooked potatoes into even cubes. Place in medium-sized bowl with celery, onion, and raisins.

In small bowl, whisk together yogurt, mayonnaise, chutney, orange juice concentrate, curry powder, and cumin. Add salt and pepper, or additional flavorings, as desired. Pour dressing over salad. Top with nuts. Serve on bed of greens, if desired.

Serves 8

Tip: To keep from mashing potatoes, use a rubber or silicon spatula to lightly and carefully fold in dressing, or plate the salad undressed, then drizzle dressing over top.

Chutney and orange juice combine to lend a sprightly, sweet-tart flavor to this unusual take on potato salad, inspired by another that was served at a now-defunct Honolulu deli. Homemade chutney is best, but Major Grey's or another store brand is fine, too. The key is to cook the potatoes to just the right degree of doneness, somewhat firm yet easily pierced with a fork. Whether you boil, bake, or microwave them, pay close attention to texture.

Japanese Soy-Braised Potatoes

4 medium-size russet potatoes

2 c. dashi (Japanese fish stock) or light chicken broth

3 Tbsp. sugar

2 ½ Tbsp. soy sauce, divided

1 clove garlic, minced

⅛ tsp. finely ground black pepper

2 Tbsp. butter

Peel potatoes; cut into bite-size pieces. Place potatoes in colander; rinse in cold, running water for a few minutes to leach out some starch. Place potatoes in saucepan with dashi or stock, sugar, 1 ½ tablespoons soy sauce, garlic, and pepper. Pot should be just large enough to accommodate them. Place drop lid on top of liquid; simmer until potatoes are tender. Remove from heat; allow to cool. Then, reheat and replace drop lid; cook until potatoes are soft and liquid is almost gone. Remove from heat; uncover; add remaining soy sauce and butter. Serve hot.

Serves 4 to 6

This hybrid dish of potatoes simmered in soy sauce and dressed with butter is representative of a culinary trend in Japan that adapts Western ideas to Asian tastes. The technique is distinctly Japanese: it incorporates a drop lid—a lid that is fitted right on top of the simmering ingredients—to seal in moisture as the liquid cooks away. The Japanese use wooden lids cut to fit their pots, but a round piece of kitchen parchment or foil laid over the liquid is equally effective.

About Dashi

Though most Islanders use powdered dashi mix (dashi-no-moto or hon-dashi), Elizabeth Andoh, perhaps the foremost English-language authority on Japanese cooking, convinced me that fresh is best—just like the superiority of homemade chicken soup over the canned variety. Both homemade versions are sweet and light, while the powdered or canned ones tend to be salty and have an odd chemical taste.

Authentic dashi is fragrantly briny—but not fishy. It requires just three ingredients: water, kombu (a dark green, dried seaweed sold in sheets), and katsuoboshi (dried bonito flakes). To make it, cut a piece of kombu to about 6-by-6 inches; wipe with damp paper towel. In saucepan, immerse kombu in 4 cups water for 20 to 30 minutes. Over medium-high heat, heat the water. When it's hot but not boiling, remove kombu, then add 2 tablespoons (about half a packet) of katsuoboshi. Bring water just to a boil; turn down heat. When flakes sink, dashi is done. Strain and use. Makes 4 cups.

Garlic Rice

2 Tbsp. olive oil

6 cloves garlic, peeled and minced

½ medium onion, thinly sliced and divided into small crescents

2 c. water

1 c. long-grain rice

In small frying pan, heat olive oil over medium-high heat, add garlic and onion; turn heat down to medium-low. Cook slowly for 30 minutes, stirring occasionally and taking care to avoid burning, until onions and garlic are mahogany-colored. Place water in saucepan and bring to a boil. Add rice and onion/garlic mixture; stir. Cover, reduce heat to medium-low, and cook 20 minutes, or until rice is tender and liquid is absorbed.

Serves 4

©iStockphoto.com/czardases

I first encountered garlic rice while reviewing a local Filipino restaurant, and I so adored it that I wrote more about it than I did the entrées! Although composed of just a few ingredients, this dish has a lovely complexity due to the long, slow caramelizing of garlic and onions. Done right, the taste is sweet and rich, so don't rush and don't stop cooking too soon—the goal is onions that are browned but not burned.

Tori Meshi/Japanese Chicken Pilaf

2 c. short-grain Japanese-style rice

2 skinless, boneless chicken breasts or 3 skinless, boneless chicken thighs

4 Tbsp. soy sauce

2 Tbsp. sugar

1 Tbsp. miso (fermented soy paste) or 1 tsp. salt

2 Tbsp. sake

1 c. boiling water

1 oz. dried matsutake or shiitake mushrooms

2 tsp. butter or vegetable oil

2 c. dashi (Japanese fish stock) or chicken broth

1/4 medium onion (about 2 oz.), sliced into very thin crescents

1 carrot, peeled, cut into 1-inch lengths, and julienned

2 oz. bamboo shoots (half an 8 oz. can, drained), sliced into thin strips

6 (about 1/2 oz.) green beans, finely chopped

Minced green onions for garnish

Place rice in pot; cover with water; set aside for 2 hours. Cut chicken into thin strips or chop roughly; marinate in soy sauce, sugar, miso, and sake for 2 hours.

Pour boiling water over dried mushrooms; rehydrate for 15 to 30 minutes. Drain, reserving mushroom water. Slice mushrooms thinly.

In large sauté pan, melt butter or heat oil; sauté chicken. Combine mushroom water and dashi or chicken broth; pour into sauté pan; bring to a boil.

Reduce heat to simmering; add rehydrated mushrooms, onions, carrots, and bamboo shoots and cook 5 to 10 minutes.

Drain rice; place in pot with liquid, chicken, and vegetables. Bring to boil; reduce heat to medium-low. Add green beans; cover. Steam 20 to 30 minutes, until rice is tender and meat and vegetables are cooked through. Garnish with green onions.

Serves 6

"Meshi" is the Japanese term for rice cooked with bits of meat, vegetables, and other flavoring ingredients. In effect, it's a pilaf or risotto, although it is steamed, not stirred, atop the stove. Use the best quality rice you can afford; the grains will be plump, unbroken, and tender. Soaking the rice in water prior to cooking is an old-fashioned technique that tenderizes the rice further and shortens the cooking time. Meshi can be a hearty side dish or an entrée.

This version is quite Westernized; if you have access to such Japanese ingredients as konnyaku (yam cake) and kamaboko (fish cake), feel free to add them.

Milho/Portuguese Polenta

2 c. rich chicken, beef, or veal stock

Salt to taste (depends on saltiness of stock or broth)

½ c. white or yellow cornmeal

2 c. thinly julienned collard greens

¼ c. minced flat-leaf parsley

2 Tbsp. butter or 1 Tbsp. cream (optional)

In Dutch oven or other large saucepan, bring stock or broth to boil. Add salt, if using; reduce heat to medium. Drizzle cornmeal slowly into boiling broth while whisking with a wire whisk to prevent lumps; as it thickens, switch to a wooden spoon. Cover; cook over low heat until thickened and cooked through, about 10 to 15 minutes. Keep warm. Just before serving, stir in collard greens, parsley, more broth if needed, and butter or cream.

Serves 4 to 6

Tip: Pour any leftovers into a loaf pan. Chill overnight. Cut into ½-inch thick slices and fry over medium heat in blend of butter and oil until golden brown and heated through. For a Portuguese breakfast, top with fried eggs, chopped parsley, chopped green or Spanish olives, and chopped fresh or roasted tomatoes.

Every Christmas and Easter, and whenever else the fancy struck her, my Portuguese grandmother served a meal of codfish stew and the thick, corn porridge called milho, a Portuguese cousin to polenta. Like rice or potatoes, milho pairs wonderfully with stews, fried fish, and grilled or braised meats. It's cheap, and it has a much-loved afterlife: leftover, chilled porridge is cut into rounds or squares and fried for breakfast the next day. (We always made extra just for this purpose.) This is a slightly fancied-up version, cooked in stock instead of water. Rightly, the original is made with couves, the large, tender leaves of Portuguese cabbage. But even in the Islands, no one sells it, so use the closest substitute, which are collard greens, or skip the cabbage and use flat-leaf parsley.

Kitchen Sink Potato-Mac Salad

1 c. salad macaroni, boiled and chilled

3 small new white or red waxy potatoes,
     peeled, boiled until tender, then chilled

1 (10 oz.) pkg. frozen peas

1 (6 oz.) can tuna or crab, drained

½ c. chopped ham or kamaboko (fish cake), chopped

2 Tbsp. minced red onion

2 stalks celery, minced

¼ c. carrot, grated

4 oz. water chestnuts, minced

3 slices fried bacon, drained and crumbled

¼ c. minced flat-leaf parsley

2 c. mayonnaise

Salt and pepper to taste

2 thinly sliced hard-boiled eggs and minced parsley for garnish

In very large bowl, combine macaroni and potatoes. In colander, pour boiling water over peas, rinse with cold water to stop the cooking, and add to macaroni mixture. Add tuna or crab; ham or kamaboko, onion, celery, carrot, water chestnuts, bacon, and parsley. With flexible spatula, fold mayonnaise into salad; add salt and pepper, as desired. Chill thoroughly. Just before serving, add additional mayonnaise, if needed, to moisten. Garnish with hard-boiled eggs and minced parsley.

Serves 8 to 10

How or why macaroni salad became integral to Island cuisine is a matter of speculation, but Hawai'i plate lunch restaurants serve variations of it by the truckload. Although I prefer a simple salad (macaroni, mayo, parsley, and a little minced Spanish olives if I'm feeling fancy), most Islanders seem to prefer what I call the "kitchen sink" type, larding their macaroni salads with everything from potatoes to canned salmon. Here's a typical kitchen sink recipe. Feel free to leave anything out—except the macaroni and mayo, of course—or add anything in.

Banana Fritters Two Ways

For the fritter batter:

1 c. all-purpose flour

2 tsp. baking powder

¼ tsp. salt

3 standard bananas or 4-5 smaller apple bananas, peeled and roughly chopped

In a medium bowl, whisk together flour, baking powder and salt; stir in bananas, mixing well to incorporate.

For savory fritters: Add ½ tsp. black pepper, ½ tsp. ground ginger, and generous pinch of cayenne powder.

For sweet dessert fritters: Do not use pepper, ginger, or cayenne. Just add 1 Tbsp. sugar.

Finish the fritters:

With ⅓-½ c. milk (nonfat is fine)

Add milk gradually, beating, to form a thickish dough, neither stiff nor soft. In sauté pan over medium-high heat, heat ¼-inch of vegetable oil until shimmering. Using two serving spoons, form small oval croquettes. Fry, turning when small holes appear in the batter, until golden-brown on all sides. Serve hot.

Makes 16 fritters (1 or 2 per serving; recipe can be halved)

Variation: Make sweet or savory fritters with peeled and crushed pineapple (drained, and juices pressed out with paper towels), or peeled and chopped apples.

At one time, fritters (fried cakes that are somewhere between flavored pancakes and croquettes) were an everyday dish, at least in Western-style households. Leftover roasts and baked fish were battered and fried for a second go-around on the dinner table, and fruits and vegetables often received the same treatment. Banana fritters are especially versatile—they can be savory to complement a main course or sweet as a dessert.

Serving Options

Savory banana fritters go well with roast pork or grilled fish, pork, or chicken.

Sweet banana fritters are sensational with vanilla ice cream. If you can find an old-fashioned rectangular box of ice cream, cut it into slices, top each slice with a hot fritter, then drizzle with chocolate or caramel sauce.

Szechuan Eggplant

4 long Japanese eggplants (about 1 ½ lb.)

1 lb. boneless pork, cut into thin strips

1 egg white

Peanut oil

2 tsp. cornstarch

2 stalks green onion, minced

1 small red chile pepper, seeded and minced

3 cloves garlic, peeled and minced

5 Tbsp. soy sauce

4 Tbsp. vinegar

1 Tbsp. sugar

No Japanese eggplant?
Use globe eggplant.

With a vegetable peeler, peel eggplant, then slice into long slices. Spray or sprinkle eggplant with water. Place on a microwave-safe plate; cover with paper towels; microwave 3 minutes. Set aside.

In bowl, combine pork and egg white. Pour 1 inch peanut oil into wok or frying pan; heat over high heat. Stir-fry pork until it changes color; remove with slotted spoon; drain on paper towels. In same hot oil, stir-fry eggplant with green onion, chile, and garlic until golden brown. Remove with slotted spoon; drain on paper towels with pork. Drain oil from pan; pour soy sauce, vinegar, and sugar into pan; bring to a boil. Return pork and eggplant to pan with sauce; cook 3 to 4 minutes.

Serves 6

Variations: Use ground pork or strips of boneless chicken; use combinations of vegetables: onions, cabbage, cauliflower, chard or other greens, bittermelon or other squash.

This traditional sweet-sour treatment of eggplant, from the cosmopolitan city of Shanghai in eastern China, isn't low-fat but it is absolutely delicious. Linda Chang Wyrgatsch, who teaches Narcissus Queen candidates to cook, taught me to microwave the eggplant instead of frying it, which saves at least a few calories!

Potluck

The Way We Party

*W*hen Islanders are invited anywhere, our first question is, "What should I bring?" Potluck in Hawai'i is an art form unto itself, so we're always looking for dishes that can be made ahead, will serve many people, and that will wow our friends and family.

"Make Plate"—Parties are Always Potluck!

Local-style parties are *always* potluck. Always. They require the strategic planning of a military campaign, but in a hang-loose kind of way—everybody pitches in seamlessly to *kōkua* (help). In turn, the hosts know their guests will return the favor. At the very least, these events start with a long, involved phone conversation about who's bringing what.

Because Island parties tend to spread like the smoke from a *huli huli* chicken sale, and because our homes are often small, many parties begin a day in advance, when some portion of the family goes to *kapu* (claim) a campsite at a public park, spending the night to assure adequate picnic tables.

As for the guests, it's assumed you'll bring your own drinks—and some extra for "moochers" or newcomers who aren't yet *ma'a* (familiar with our ways). It's also assumed you'll bring something for the *pūpū* table, as well as something for dinner, and maybe a dessert too—all packed in a coffin-size cooler prominently marked with your name so as to distinguish it from the other dozen coolers there.

You'll wear a T-shirt and slippers, maybe with a bathing suit underneath. You'll shuck off your slippers at the back door and march into the kitchen calling "hoooo-ey" to announce your presence. If it's a birthday, you'll bring a lei. If it's a wedding, you'll bring cash or a check for the calabash bowl. If you play an instrument, you'll bring it along. If you dance hula, you'll be ready to be called on.

You'll sit on the folding chairs your host keeps stacked in the garage, and, if the party isn't at a beach park with a blue tarp tied to a coconut tree for shade, you'll almost certainly sit in the carport—the universal second living room of the Islands.

When it's time for dinner, you'll eat off paper plates, and then you'll use more paper plates (or perhaps the disposable plastic containers you brought) to "make plate" for yourself—and anybody in your family who didn't get to come to the party. Everybody takes something home; everybody helps collect the beer bottles; and everybody sacks up the rubbish.

Mahalos (thank yous) come in the form of shared work, for whoever helped you at this party will call on you for help at their next party. And that, as my old friend Maili Yardley would say, is, "The Island Way."

(Note: serving sizes given in the recipes that follow are by necessity approximates—there's no telling what size portions people may take!)

Kalakoa Rice Casserole

1 c. red jasmine rice, brown sweet rice, or wild rice

2 c. white rice (long-grain is best)

2 slices bacon

1 lb. Portuguese sausage, minced

1 medium onion, chopped

2 sweet red, yellow or orange peppers, chopped

½ lb. mushrooms, sliced

Half bunch flat-leaf parsley, minced

2 (10 ¾ oz.) cans cream of mushroom soup

Milk

Freshly ground black pepper

Steam red, brown or wild rice according to package directions. Separately, steam white rice according to package directions. In frying pan, fry bacon until crisp; remove; drain on paper towels; chop or crumble. In same pan, fry Portuguese sausage until cooked through and slightly crisp; remove; drain well on paper towels; chop or crumble. In same pan, with most of the fat poured out, sauté onions, peppers, mushrooms, and parsley over medium heat until onions are limp and translucent. Drain on paper towels.

In large bowl, combine cooked rice, bacon, Portuguese sausage, and vegetables. Add mushroom soup and 2 cans milk; stir well. Season with freshly ground pepper. (Bacon, sausage, and soup provide plenty of salt). Spread in 9-by-13-inch casserole dish and bake at 350 degrees until liquid is absorbed, 50 to 60 minutes.

Serves 8 to 10

Kalakoa is a pidgin English word that means "multicolored," a Hawaiianization of the word calico. This multicolored casserole of rice, meats, and vegetables is delicious whether hot or at room temperature and can be altered to suit your tastes.
For example, make it a southwestern-style dish by adding chorizo and oregano. Substitute ham, or fried, crumbled bacon, for sausage; use a cheese soup instead of mushroom soup. Add frozen peas or fresh or frozen spinach to the vegetable mixture and vary the types of mushrooms.

Empañadas Casserole

2 tsp. olive oil

1 medium onion, chopped

3-4 cloves garlic, minced

3 lb. skinless, boneless chicken (mixed breasts and thighs)

3 medium russet potatoes, peeled and cubed

1 c. water

1 tsp. dried oregano (more, if desired)

1 tsp. ground cumin (more, if desired)

1 tsp. salt

1 tsp. black pepper

4 oz. cream cheese, cut into in small chunks

2 c. grated Jack or other white cheese

¾ c. pimento-stuffed green olives, chopped

1 uncooked double-crust pastry

In large sauté pan, heat olive oil. Sauté onion and garlic until limp and translucent. Cut chicken breasts in quarters so pieces are same size as thighs. Place chicken, cubed potatoes, water, and spices in pan with onion and garlic. Cook about 20 minutes, until chicken is cooked through, potatoes are tender, and liquid is cooked off. With tongs, place chicken in 9-by-13-inch baking dish, and use two forks to shred. Return chicken to saucepan; add cheeses and olives. Stir to combine all ingredients; correct seasonings. Pour filling into baking dish; set aside. Preheat oven to 400 degrees. On floured surface, roll out pastry crust to roughly 9-by-13 inches. Place crust over filling. Finish by scalloping edges or rolling them inward. Bake 25 to 30 minutes, until golden on top and filling bubbles.

Serves 12; more if cut in smaller, appetizer-sized pieces

> I love empañadas, the spicy meat-stuffed pastries of Central and South America, but making individual turnovers is a lot of work. For a Dia de los Muertos (Day of the Dead) party, I devised this much easier version: empañadas stuffing packed into a casserole and topped with pie crust. (Frozen or crust mix is fine.)

Teriyaki Beef Sticks

1 tsp. salt

½ c. brown sugar

⅓ c. soy sauce

2 cloves garlic

2-inch slice fresh ginger

2 lb. beef, sliced paper-thin

Bamboo skewers

In bowl, combine salt, brown sugar, soy sauce. Peel garlic and ginger and smash by placing Chinese cleaver on top of them and striking hard with fist. Add garlic and ginger to soy sauce mixture. Place beef in marinade; marinate at least 1 hour (overnight is ideal). One hour before cooking, soak bamboo skewers in water so they won't burn. Drain beef well, thread in-and-out ribbon fashion on skewers, and either grill over charcoal, broil on rack, or fry in frying pan.

Serves 4 (may be multiplied as many times as needed to feed a crowd)

Variation 1: If you're serving a large group, don't bother with skewers: just grill or broil, being careful not to overcook, as the beef gets tough quickly. Place beef on serving dish. Place marinade in saucepan; bring to full rolling boil; drizzle marinade over meat.

Variation 2: Substitute strips of skinless, boneless chicken thighs.

These are an Island standard: thin-sliced beef, marinated in a sweet-salty mixture, grilled, broiled, or fried, then served over rice or atop a steaming bowl of saimin (Japanese noodle soup). Islanders prefer a marinade so sweet it almost candies the beef; you'll see the meat change color and become shiny. (Food science tells us that a salt-sugar brine untangles protein, tenderizing and moisturizing the meat.)

To make beef sticks, you need bamboo skewers and the right cut of beef: well-marbled eye of round or a similar cut, sliced literally paper-thin. (Have the butcher cut it for you if it's not readily available.) Thread the slices on skewers in an alternating ribbon before grilling or broiling.

Chirashi-zushi/Tossed Sushi

Vegetable oil or cooking spray

4 eggs

3 tsp. sugar

¼ tsp. salt

4 c. sushi rice*

½ c. peas or chopped sugar snap peas, blanched

1 c. ham or SPAM, cut into strips

1 medium carrot, cut into strips and blanched

2 oz. dried shiitake mushrooms, reconstituted in hot water and cut into strips

2-3 Tbsp. *furikake (Japanese condiment usually sprinkled over rice)*

Oil a frying pan; heat over medium-high heat. Beat eggs with sugar and salt; pour into frying pan, and reduce heat to low. Allow to cook in a thin layer until solid. Turn out onto cutting board; cut into strips. Spread rice in large, flat, casserole dish or platter. Over top, scatter scrambled eggs, peas, ham or Spam, carrot, mushrooms, and *furikake*. Cool. Cover with plastic wrap until serving time.

Serves 8 to 10

* See p. 27, Pūpū chapter, for sushi rice recipe.

> Making sushi is an art form, but anyone can assemble a dish of chirashi-zushi (scattered sushi), a simple dish of seasoned rice topped with various sushi condiments: strips of omelet, crunchy vegetables, meats, or fish.

©iStockphoto.com/Branislav Senic

Kelaguen Manok/Chamorro Chicken Ceviche

2 skinless, boneless chicken breasts

¾-1 c. freshly squeezed lemon juice (about 6 lemons)

½-1 c. freshly grated coconut

2 ½ Tbsp. minced green onions, white and green parts

1-3 (about 1 tsp.) small, hot, red chiles, minced, to taste

Salt and pepper to taste

Preheat broiler. Cut chicken breasts in half crosswise, butterfly open. Broil 3 to 5 minutes per side, just until done but still moist. Cool, then put in a food processor and pulse until minced or mince by hand. In a bowl, lightly toss together chicken, lemon juice, coconut, green onions, and chiles with a plastic spatula. If desired, season with salt and pepper and add additional lemon or coconut. Allow to marinate at room temperature 1 hour before serving.

Serves 4 to 6

No fresh coconut?
Use unsweetened, dehydrated coconut moistened with coconut milk.

The first time I tasted Chicken *Kelaguen*, as leftovers from a party given by a friend whose husband is Chamorro, I literally had no idea what it was. Fish? Meat? What combination of ingredients produced such an explosion of piquant flavor and chewy texture? When I found out how easy it was to make, I was delighted.

Okazuya-style Tuna Cakes

1 lb. fresh tuna or *aku*

2 tsp. garlic salt

1 Tbsp. minced garlic

2 tsp. finely grated ginger

½ tsp. sesame oil

½ tsp. fresh-ground black pepper

1 egg, beaten

2 Tbsp. fine, dry bread crumbs or panko (Japanese bread crumbs)

Oil for frying (vegetable or olive)

Cut fish into chunks. In food processor, pulse fish briefly, making sure it remains chunky. In medium bowl, combine fish and remaining ingredients (except oil). For appetizers, form into 10 to 12 small balls; for larger servings, form into 4 to 6 hamburger-sized patties. Preheat oven to its lowest temperature.

> A common offering in Island okazuya (Japanese delicatessens) is fish patties made from the scraped flesh of bony trash fish. A few delis serve a gourmet version made from minced, fresh 'ahi (yellowfin or bigeye tuna) or less expensive *aku* (skipjack tuna), a rich, red-fleshed fish similar to mackerel.

In sauté pan, heat oil over medium-high heat until hot and shimmering. Frying in batches so croquettes or patties are not crowded, place fish cakes in oil. Reduce heat to medium and fry 2 to 4 minutes per side, until golden brown and cooked through.

Place fish cakes on paper towels on heatproof dish; place dish in warm oven while remaining cakes fry. Serve hot as an entrée with sweet chile or tartar sauce, or at room temperature as an appetizer.

Serves 4 to 6 (entrée) or 10 to 12 (appetizer)

Variations: Use peeled raw shrimp in place of tuna. Add up to ¼ cup grated carrot, French-sliced green beans, chopped water chestnuts, bamboo shoots, or peeled and parboiled chopped gobo (burdock root).

Marylene Chun's awesome tartar sauce: ½ cup mayonnaise, 1 teaspoon finely minced raw onion, 1 tablespoon pickle relish.

Chap Chae/Korean Celebration Noodles

3 Tbsp. sherry, divided

3 Tbsp. soy sauce, divided

3 Tbsp. sesame oil, divided

1 ½ Tbsp. lemon juice

2 Tbsp. sugar

2 Tbsp. minced garlic

1 ½ lb. lean beef tenderloin, in strips, sliced along the grain

2-3 Tbsp. vegetable oil, divided

10 dried shiitake mushrooms, reconstituted in hot water, drained and julienned

2-3 c. mixed julienned vegetables: spinach, Napa cabbage, onion, carrot, scallion, bell pepper (any color)

3 cloves garlic, crushed

10-12 oz. dang myun (sweet potato noodles)

2 Tbsp. toasted pine nuts

Pinch of hot red pepper flakes or Korean coarse red pepper powder (as for kim chee)

In bowl, combine 1 tablespoon sherry, 1 tablespoon soy sauce, 1 tablespoon sesame oil, lemon juice, sugar, and 2 tablespoons minced garlic. Place beef in bowl and work marinade into it with your fingers. Marinate for 10 minutes. In wok, heat 1 tablespoon of vegetable oil. Place beef and marinade in wok and stir-fry until beef is cooked through. Place beef in large bowl; set aside.

Place 1 tablespoon of vegetable oil in wok, heat, and stir-fry all vegetables (in batches if your wok isn't large) making sure they remain brightly colored and crisp. Add remaining sherry and soy sauce, 1 tablespoon sesame oil, and 3 cloves crushed garlic. Stir-fry a few seconds, then place in bowl with beef. Bring large pot of water to boil, place noodles inside, and boil 5 minutes, until softened but still al dente. Drain; plunge into cold water to stop cooking. Toss with remaining sesame oil. Place in bowl and toss all ingredients together, garnishing with pine nuts and pepper flakes. Serve at room temperature.

Serves 6 to 8

No sweet potato noodles? Use any transparent cellophane-type noodle, rice or mung bean.

It is impossible for Koreans to celebrate without a platter of chap chae, transparent noodles glistening with a soy-based sauce flecked with vegetable strips. The dish is compiled—ingredient-by-stir-fried-ingredient—in a large bowl, then served at room temperature.

My Best Baked Spare Ribs

For the marinade:

½ c. apricot or pineapple jam

¼ c. Thai sweet chile sauce

⅓ c. soy sauce

⅓ c. cider vinegar

⅓ c. tahini (sesame butter)

2 tsp. fresh grated ginger

2 cloves garlic, minced

1 tsp. dry mustard

1 Tbsp. sugar

3 Tbsp. dry sherry

2 Tbsp. minced green onion

In large bowl, with a rubber spatula and then with a whisk: combine jam, chile sauce, soy sauce, vinegar, tahini, ginger, garlic, mustard, sugar, sherry, and green onions. This marinade can be assembled a day ahead and held in an airtight container in the refrigerator.

For the ribs:

4-4 ½ lb. pork sparerib rack

Hawaiian or kosher salt

1 onion, sliced

½ lemon, thin-sliced

2 Tbsp. toasted sesame seeds and minced green onion, both for garnish

Islanders just love ribs! I have yet to see a community cookbook that doesn't have a recipe for pork spareribs or beef short ribs—or both. There are three schools of Island rib recipes: the sweet-sour fans (generally a marinade of vinegar, sugar, pineapple), the tangy-spicy tomato contingent (ketchup or tomato sauce with sugar, vinegar, and spices), and the Japanese-stylists (soy sauce, ginger, and sugar).

I've experimented with a lot of recipes, but this one—a marriage of many ideas I've encountered over the years—is my favorite. It uses a full rack of pork spareribs, usually about thirteen well-marbled and meaty ribs.

Cut sparerib rack in two or three pieces (size that will fit your largest pot). Place in pot, cover with water, add generous pinch of salt. Bring to boil; simmer 20 minutes. Drain, place ribs in large casserole or baking dish, and pour marinade over. Marinate 1 to 5 hours. Preheat oven to 350 degrees. Arrange onion and lemon over ribs, place ribs in oven. Bake for 3 hours, periodically spooning marinade over ribs, until meat is tender and falling from bone. Garnish with toasted sesame seeds and minced green onion before serving.

Serves 4 to 6 generously

Variation: To get a good glaze, bake 2 ½ hours, then finish on a grill (white-ash stage if you're using briquettes; medium heat if gas).

Portable Lū'au

How to Host a Hawaiian-style Feast—No Matter Where You Live

©IHP Archive

*T*he Hawaiian feast we call a lū'au (properly a *pā'ina*) was christened about one hundred years ago to honor the taro leaves, or lū'au. Hawaiians consider *kalo*, also called taro, to be their mythological parent—according to Hawaiian creation legends, the taro plant is the first child of the mother and father gods.

Some forms of taro are invariable features of an Island-style menu: the boiled lū'au leaf, the baked corm (similar to a root), or poi, the thick, custard-textured mixture that is a core food of the Hawaiian diet.

Although the standard lū'au menu is considered Hawaiian, it's really a mix of dishes that incorporate a range of ethnic influences: Chinese (chicken long rice), Japanese (steamed rice, certain forms of *poke*), and Caucasian (the cake often served for dessert).

Today, it's difficult to give a truly authentic *pā'ina*, even in Hawai'i. Many foods are scarce and techniques for preparing them little understood. And, to be honest, dishes like intestine stew and salted fish guts have lost broad appeal.

However, you can readily recreate the most beloved lū'au dishes in a home kitchen. Plus, we offer suggestions on substitutions for ingredients that may be difficult to locate and for good mail-order sources of Hawaiian foods.

At the very least, a typical lū'au features *laulau*, *kālua* pork, chicken long rice, *lomi* salmon, poi, baked sweet potatoes, steamed rice, and *haupia* (coconut pudding) and/or cake. Other common dishes include chicken or squid lū'au, *poke*, and *lawelu* fish (fish baked in ti leaves). However, pretty much anything goes today—from macaroni salad to ice cream.

Once your menu is set, you'll want to turn your attention to creating a lū'au atmosphere.

Creating a Lū'au Atmosphere

Lei. Ideally, everyone at a lū'au is greeted with a lei. At the very least, guests of honor and elders should be so adorned. If lei aren't readily available, make your own with fresh flowers, order artificial ones, or, if you're crafty, crochet rather realistic versions.

To make fresh flower lei, use a long, thin craft needle. Thread with about two yards of thin cotton thread or crochet yarn; double and knot the thread. Cut the stem just below flower, and pierce flower through the center. Mainland flowers you can use include carnations, roses, stock, chrysanthemums, dahlias, fuschia, stock, and jasmine. Tie ends. Place lei in flat boxes or trays; cover with damp paper towels; refrigerate until lū'au time. The easiest to make, carnation lei, can be refreshed by immersing in cool water; shaking them out; and refrigerating as above. These lei will keep for days.

Greet guests at door with lei (place a lei over the guest's head and offer a *honi*, a kiss of friendly affection on the cheek). Or, in keeping with the old-style, drape a lei over the back of each chair at the table; escort guests to their seats; then, present the lei.

Table décor. Traditionally, lū'au were served on long, narrow mats on the ground, with guests seated cross-legged around the spread. Today, a long, narrow table with chairs is customary. Tables may be covered with cloth or white paper. Greenery is arranged down the center (usually ferns or ti leaves), and flowers are scattered randomly along the greenery. Bouquets or centerpieces are not customary.

Even on the Mainland, you can often get ti leaves from florists. Or use whatever greens you have in your yard, such as ivy or philodendron. You can also purchase artificial greens.

Table settings. In old-style lū'au, each place is set with a small wooden plate of raw onion, Hawaiian salt (kosher salt is a good substitute), and *'inamona* (see recipe p. 126). Calabashes (wooden bowls) of poi are placed between every few settings. It is also common for plates of cut-up cake and *haupia* to be placed along the table and eaten at the meal's end. Shaker bottles of soy sauce and chile pepper water (a common Island condiment) are often provided.

Food is generally served buffet-style with guests queuing up and picking up their plates. However, if you are serving a smaller group, food can be plated, or passed, family-style.

Island dress. At one time, mu'umu'u or *holokū* (long, voluminous Mother Hubbard-style gowns, the latter having a train and generally a ruffled hem) were de rigueur for a lū'au. Men wore white tuxedo shirts, cummerbunds, and black pants. This convention has relaxed to the point of being nonexistent. Today, any form of alohawear is acceptable—from aloha shirts and jeans to flowered sundresses.

Kāhea 'ai! You are called to eat.

Can't Find It?

What to use in place of traditional ingredients:

- Lū'au/taro leaf: canned spinach
- Hawaiian salt: kosher salt
- Hawaiian chiles: any small, hot red chile
- *Kukui* nuts: macadamia nuts
- Ti leaves: kitchen parchment
- Salt salmon: Northwestern smoked salmon (not lox)
- Poi: Sorry, there's no substitute—but you can make it or order it

Still Can't Find It? Lū'au by Mail

Try these sources for lū'au foods, lei, ti leaves, and other Hawaiian party supplies:

- www.1stluau.com—Frozen, pre-cooked lū'au foods, char siu and Portuguese sausage, fresh or nut lei. 888-441-5828.
- www.luauking.com—Lū'au packages, Hawai'i seafood, accessories, lei. 1-877-582-8546.

Got Poi?

Poi can be purchased dried for reconstituting with water, but most agree that this product is only for the desperate.

If there is an Asian, African, Caribbean, Filipino, Polynesian, or South American population where you live, you can find taro in the stores that serve these folks. Common names include *kalo*, *talo*, or *dalo* (Polynesia); *imo* or *satoimo* (Japan); dasheen (West Indies); *gabi* (Philippines); and malanga (Caribbean). If you can get your hands on taro, you can make poi at home.

Smaller taro corms can be cooked whole and unpeeled. To speed cooking of larger corms (bigger than a standard new potato or small russet), peel and cut into chunks. (When handling raw taro, wear gloves to protect your hands from the irritating calcium oxalate crystals in the plants.)

To boil: In large saucepan, cover with water, and boil 60 to 90 minutes until a knife easily pierces to the center.

To microwave: Peel and slice, place in microwavable dish, and drizzle with water. Cover and microwave on high, frequently checking for doneness (until taro can be pierced easily with a fork).

To bake: Place washed corms in 375-degree oven for 60 to 90 minutes. Peel under running water with vegetable peeler, then cut into cubes. Measure taro: you need equal parts water to taro. Set water aside to use in mashing.

To mash taro (which should still be warm): put it through ricer, grinder, or juicer; use a potato masher; or process in blender or food processor. As you mash, gradually drizzle in water. Press half-finished poi through a fine strainer or several thicknesses of cheesecloth to remove lumps. Continue adding water to achieve desired consistency.

Finished poi can be stored on the countertop or in the refrigerator, but the surface must be covered with a little water to prevent "skin" from forming.

How thick or thin you make the poi and how long to age it before eating is a matter of personal preference. Most people like it about the thickness of pudding and about a day or two old.

Kālua Pork/Smoky Pork Roast

3 Tbsp. Hawaiian or kosher salt

¼ c. soy sauce

¼ c. vegetable oil

¼-½ tsp. smoky seasoning (Liquid Smoke, if available)

4-5 lb. boneless, well-marbled pork roast (i.e. pork butt roast, boneless blade)

2 bay leaves, broken into several pieces

2 cloves garlic, smashed, broken into several pieces

Preheat oven to 375 degrees. In very large bowl, combine salt, soy sauce, vegetable oil, and smoky seasoning. Place pork roast in bowl; slash rather deeply all over; roll thoroughly in seasonings.

On flat work surface, lay out two long pieces of heavy-duty aluminum foil in a cross shape. (If using ti leaves, lay about 8 of them in a spiral.) Place roast in center of the cross; pour over remaining seasonings; scatter bay leaves and garlic over roast. (Fold over ti leaves, if using.) Wrap in foil.

Place a steaming rack, or several large, crumpled balls of aluminum foil, in a large Dutch oven. Place foil-wrapped roast on top, and pour in enough boiling water to cover bottom of pot, yet not so much that water touches roast. Cover.

Place roast in oven; roast 1 hour per pound. Check water level each hour, replenishing water as needed.

Roast is done when fully cooked, moist, and falling apart. Remove from oven; allow to settle, covered, for 10 to 15 minutes. Shred with two forks. Serve.

Serves 8 to 10

Advance preparation: Kālua pork may be made days or weeks in advance, frozen, and reheated. Defrost and warm gently in oven or microwave.

Slow-cooker method: After slashing roast and combining it with seasonings, place roast in crockpot, and add 1 cup water. Cook on low for 12 to 15 hours (overnight), checking periodically to be sure liquid has not completely evaporated.

Kālua—literally, "to bake in an earth oven"—is the centerpiece of any feast. Meats, fish, vegetables, and even fruits, such as cooking bananas, are prepared in an *imu*, which is an earthen pit lined with red-hot rocks and damp banana leaves (or, in modern times, chicken wire and wet burlap). The fine-textured rocks that draw in heat without cracking are treasured family heirlooms.

It would not be a lū'au without *kālua* pork wrapped in ti leaves (if they're available), and shredded before serving. Luckily, ti leaves are optional, and an oven or a crockpot is a more-than-adequate substitute. A few drops (but not too much!) of a smoky seasoning, such as Liquid Smoke, mimic the characteristic infusion of smokiness lent by the *imu*.

Kālua pork makes a great sandwich and is used in many appetizers.

Laulau/Steamed Pork and Fish Bundles

For each *laulau*:

4-6 ti leaves

2-3 taro leaves (lūʻau leaves)

5-6 oz. well-marbled pork (pork butt or boneless blade roast)

2 oz. oily fish, such as black cod, salmon, mackerel (optional)

¼-½ tsp. Hawaiian or kosher salt

1 oz. salt pork (1 crosswise slice)

Place 15-inch length of heavy-duty aluminum foil on flat surface; arrange ti leaves in spiral on top, or use a 5-inch length of kitchen parchment, and place taro leaves over both. Place pork and fish in center; scatter Hawaiian salt over; place salt pork on top. Fold in leaves to form a bundle; repeat with parchment, then foil. Place bundles in steamer basket. Steam, covered, over simmering water 4 to 5 hours (the more *laulau*, the longer the steaming time). Check every half hour; add boiling water as needed.

Makes 1 *laulau*; repeat as often as desired

Tip: A rice cooker with a steamer plate is perfect for cooking *laulau*; just be sure to refresh with boiling water every hour or so.

Moist, piquant, and meltingly tender, *laulau*—steamed bundles of meat, fish, and vegetables—are always served at lūʻau. (*Laulau* is actually a technique, not a dish: it means to steam-roast a food in a wrapped bundle. Bundles are traditionally made of ti (or sometimes banana) leaves laid in a cross or spiral, with the ingredients placed in the center. The ends of the ti are drawn up and the tips and stems are tied together to form a packet. The bundles are placed in the *imu* (earth oven) or steamed over boiling water or in a pressure cooker. (The leaves serve as a wrapper, but are not eaten—kitchen parchment is an excellent substitute, supplemented by aluminum foil.)

Laulau may be stuffed with any meat, fish, or vegetable that stands up well to long, slow cooking. Pork, salt fish, and taro leaves are standard, but beef, fresh fish, and sweet potatoes or yams also appear.

No ti or taro leaves? Use 2 to 4 pieces of kale or collards in place of ti (trim stems, then slit central rib part-way through to make it more flexible). Instead of lūʻau leaves, use about one-third can spinach leaves (well drained) per *laulau*, along with pork and fish. (Unlike ti leaves, kale and collards are edible.)

Chicken Lū'au/Coconut Milk Ragout

3 Tbsp. butter, divided

1 ½ lb. skinless, boneless chicken thighs, cut into bite-size pieces

½ medium onion, chopped

2 Tbsp. flour

1 (13 ½ oz.) can coconut milk

1 c. milk

½ c. chicken broth

1 pkg. lū'au leaves, boiled and drained or 2 cans spinach, drained

Salt and pepper to taste

In a large, open frying pan or Dutch oven, melt 1 tablespoon butter and brown chicken pieces. Place chicken pieces in ovenproof casserole. Brown onions in butter; place in casserole. In the original pan, melt remaining 2 tablespoons butter; whisk in flour and cook for 1 minute, stirring constantly. Whisk in coconut milk, milk, and chicken broth, cooking until slightly thickened. Pour white sauce into casserole. Add spinach or lū'au leaves; add salt and pepper as needed. Bake at 375 degrees for 30 minutes. Serve this rich stew piping hot.

Serves 8 to 10

Lū'au stew combines lū'au leaves or spinach, coconut milk, and chicken or squid. This streamlined version turns the dish into a rich, oven ragout.

Taro leaves are highly nutritious and believed to convey many health benefits. In the Islands, the leaves are sold in one-pound bags of about a dozen leaves each. Since they contain oxalic acid crystals that can severely irritate the mouth and throat, the leaves must be immersed in water and boiled until fully cooked, usually forty minutes to one hour.

©IHP Archive

Poke Steak

1 lb. flank steak, trimmed of fat and slashed across the grain

1 c. bottled teriyaki sauce

1 medium sweet onion (Maui, Vidalia or other), julienned

1 large, vine-ripened tomato

1 Tbsp. chopped garlic

1 Tbsp. chopped fresh ginger

1 Tbsp. macadamia nut relish (see recipe p. 126)

1 Tbsp. sesame oil

1 Tbsp. patis (fish sauce)

1 Tbsp. sambal oelek (red chile paste)

½ c. thinly sliced green onions (green part only)

In 9-by-13-inch baking dish, marinate flank steak in teriyaki sauce. Prepare charcoal or gas grill, or pre-heat oven broiler. Sear meat, broiling or grilling 4 minutes per side, until pink in center and caramelized on outside. Slice across grain, cutting into thin, short slivers. In serving bowl, combine remaining ingredients and toss with flank steak. May be held a short time in refrigerator, but warm to room temperature before serving.

Serves 8 as an appetizer

No sambal oelek? Use any chile paste; a dash or two of hot sauce; or some cayenne.

©iStockphoto.com/Robert Simon

In Hawaiian tradition, *poke* is chunks of raw fish flavored with a salt-nut relish and crunchy fresh seaweed. But today, *poke* bars in supermarkets and fish shops showcase infinite variations influenced by the Islands' many ethnicities: *poke* flavored with Korean kim chee, or Japanese soy and sesame, or Southeast Asian red chile paste, or Filipino fish sauce, as well as *poke* made with cooked shrimp, raw crab, and even chunks of deep-fried tofu.

During a contemporary lū'au some years ago at the Ritz-Carlton Kapalua, Chef Patrick Callerac, the French expatriate who owns the Maui bistro Chez Paul, created this innovation: *poke* made from seared flank steak. I begged the recipe from him and have been serving it ever since. It's particularly appealing to those who might shy away from raw fish. Patrick kindly offered his permission to share it here.

Contemporary ʻInamona/Macadamia Nut Relish

½ c. (2 ½ oz.) roasted, salted macadamia nuts

Generous pinch or two Hawaiian salt or *ʻalaea* red salt

2 or more small, hot, fresh, minced red chiles (remove seeds to temper heat, if desired)

Combine ingredients in mortar bowl; stir; then pound with pestle, breaking nuts into small pieces. Store in airtight container in refrigerator up to one month.

Serves 8

©iStockphoto.com/Norman Chan

ʻInamona, made by combining roasted *kukui* nuts (candlenuts) with sea salt, was a favorite condiment of Hawaiians. *Kukui* nuts are mild-flavored and extremely oily, while the macadamia nuts used here are a richer-tasting, more readily available substitute. The key to this recipe is pounding the relish. Hawaiians used a wooden bowl and a stone; I prefer a large, stone, Thai-style mortar and pestle.

When chiles—*nīoi* in Hawaiian—were introduced after Western contact (possibly via the Spanish or Portuguese), these inch-long fingers of fiery red or yellow peppers were so appreciated they came to be called "Hawaiian peppers."

Hawaiians are fond of tempering rich foods with sharper flavored ones (like that of raw onion, flaked salt, and chiles); and also of using bland or sour foods (such as poi, breadfruit, and even a form of poi made with mashed banana) to cut fat or salt. This relish will be used for similar effect so, to serve its purpose, prepare it as salty and spicy as you can stand it!

Chicken Long Rice/Gingered Chicken Stew

1 pkg. (3 ¾ oz.) bean threads

4 c. rich chicken broth

2 c. water

1 ½ lb. skinless, boneless chicken thighs, cut into chunks

1 ½ lb. skinless, boneless chicken breast, cut into chunks

2 carrots, peeled, cut into 1 ½-inch shoestrings

4-inch piece (about 1 ½ oz.) ginger, peeled and sliced

4 (about 3 oz.) fresh shiitake mushrooms, cut in half crosswise and sliced

Dash Chinese 5-spice powder

½ tsp. salt

1 Tbsp. soy sauce

½ c. green onions, cut into 1-inch lengths

In medium bowl, pour hot water over bean threads; cover until softened (about 10 minutes). Drain. With scissors, snip into bite-size lengths. Set aside.

In soup pot, combine broth and water. Add chicken; heat to simmer. Add carrots and ginger; simmer 10 minutes. Add mushrooms, bean threads; 5-spice powder, salt, and soy sauce; simmer another 15 to 20 minutes, until chicken is cooked through and flavors meld. Garnish with green onions.

Serves 8

Here's a quick version of a Chinese stew that has become standard lū'au fare. Gingery, nutritious, and filling, it's often served over a scoop of steamed rice. The bean thread noodles (also known as sai fun, cellophane threads, or glass noodles) lend a pleasing chewiness to the dish.

Lomi Salmon/Salmon Tomato Salad

8 oz. salt salmon or Northwest Indian-style smoked salmon

3 large, ripe tomatoes, seeded and chopped*

1 small sweet onion, peeled and minced

2 stalks green onions, minced (green part only)

2-4 cubes ice, crushed

If using salt salmon, place in bowl; cover with boiling water for 10 minutes to leach out salt. Drain and taste—if still too salty, repeat. If using smoked salmon, no preparation is necessary.

In shallow, open bowl, *lomi* the salmon, breaking it apart by massaging it into flakes with your fingers. Remove bones. Add seeded and chopped tomatoes; minced onion; and green onion. Place ice on top; massage; turn the entire mixture together in your hands. Refrigerate at least one-half hour before serving.

Serves 8

No salt salmon?
Use Northwest Indian-style smoked salmon (not lox).

* *Tip:* To seed tomato, cut in half crosswise. Working over sink, squeeze tomato firmly in one hand, shaking to free seeds; use fingers to free any large seed deposits.

Lomi salmon has an interesting history: Salmon don't frequent Hawaiian waters, but salt salmon, as prepared by Northwest Indian tribes, was introduced to Hawaiʻi in the 1800s by Hudson's Bay Company ships that began selling lightweight, nutritious products to ship's chandlers in Honolulu. How or when salt salmon became a local favorite is not recorded. Hawaiians had long preserved fish by means of salting, and it's likely that salmon's popularity stemmed, in part, from its oil-rich texture and appealing flavor.

Lomi salmon, since it's both expensive and intensely flavored, is more of an appetite teaser or a condiment than a salad, yet it refreshes as a salad does during a rich meal. In Hawaiian, *"lomi"* means to massage.

Old-Fashioned Prune Cake

1 ½ c. dried, pitted prunes	1 ½ tsp. cinnamon
2 ¾ c. flour	1 ½ tsp. baking soda, divided
½ tsp. salt	1 c. butter, softened
½ tsp. cloves	1 ½ c. sugar
1 tsp. nutmeg	3 eggs
½ tsp. mace	¾ cup boiling hot coffee

Preheat oven to 375 degrees—350 degrees if using a glass baking dish. Grease 9-by-13-inch baking pan or spray with oil-flour baking spray. Set aside. Place prunes in food processor; chop; set aside. In medium bowl, whisk together flour, salt, cloves, nutmeg, mace, cinnamon, and ½ teaspoon baking soda. Cream butter with electric or standing mixer. Add sugar; cream until light-colored and fluffy. Add eggs; beat until incorporated.

In small bowl or measuring cup, combine remaining baking soda and coffee. Alternately add dry ingredients and coffee mixture to batter, beating well between additions. Stir in prunes. Turn batter into prepared baking dish. Bake about 30 minutes or until center springs back when lightly touched and toothpick inserted into center comes out clean. Cool and frost as desired.

Serves 8 generously

A cake may seem an odd choice for a chapter on Hawaiian feasts, yet at some point (probably in the early twentieth century), cakes became fixtures on lū'au tables and they continue to be today. Old-timers recall that there were usually several flavors of cake—coconut, prune, angelfood—cut into single-serving squares and arranged randomly on plates or cake stands in the center of long lū'au tables. The squares were topped liberally with icing, either a boiled seven-minute white icing or fruited butter frosting. In the old days, dried and canned fruits, which were relatively inexpensive and widely available, were used to keep the confections moist.

Old-style prune cake recipes often call for stewed prunes or instructed you to stew dried prunes before using. However, today's vacuum-packed dried prunes are so tender that no stewing is needed. For a special occasion, this cake can be baked in three round layers, but for lū'aus, sheet cakes are traditional (and easier). As with many old-time cake recipes, this one calls for mace, made from the outer coating of the nutmeg. It's hard to find these days, so feel free to supplement with additional nutmeg.

Two Traditions

Seven-minute Icing: In the top of a double boiler over simmering (not boiling) water, combine 2 egg whites, 1 cup sugar, 3 tablespoons water, and ½ teaspoon cream of tartar. Beat with an electric mixer about 7 minutes, until whites stand in peaks. Use as is or stir in 1 cup chopped prunes.

Butter-fruit Frosting: Beat together 2 cups softened butter and 2 cups sifted confectioners' sugar. Drain 1 cup canned fruit (apricots, peaches, pineapple, prunes, dates), then mash. Stir into butter mixture. *Caution:* This frosting has *no* staying power on warm, humid days. For a bit more stability and an interesting flavor, substitute 8 ounces softened cream cheese for 1 cup butter.

©iStockphoto.com/George Bailey

Cracking The Coconut

Let's take a step back to the time when every Islander had access to free coconuts—if not from their own trees, then from a neighbor's bounty—either green or brown.

• Green coconuts provide coconut juice or spoon meat. Coconut juice is the liquid that sloshes around when you shake a young coconut; spoon meat is the early stage of the fruit, when it's still custard-soft.

• Brown coconuts provide coconut meat to shave, chop, or grate for use in recipes. There might be a little coconut juice or water in the nut. Husked brown coconuts are found in stores that supply Polynesian, Caribbean, and other ethnic communities. When cracked, the coconut should smell sweet. If the smell is rancid, it's spoiled. Discard it.

©iStockphoto.com/Michael Valdez

Cracking A Coconut

Husk. If husk is still on, peel it off by slamming the coconut on a concrete surface. Alternate pointed and rounded ends until the fiber begins to degrade, then pull off the husk.

Pierce and bake. Wear oven mitts and use a Phillips screwdriver to pierce at least two of the "eyes" and pour out juice. Place husked coconut in a 325-degree oven for 30 minutes.

Crack. If you feel confident with a machete, use its back side (not sharp end) to crack the nut, working around the equator of the nut, until it cracks in two pieces. Otherwise, wrap the nut in a towel and hit with hammer; working around the perimeter until it cracks.

The meat. Use a strong, thin-bladed knife to pry coconut chunks out of shell; peel off brown part with sharp vegetable peeler. Then chop, shave, or grate coconut meat. One coconut yields about ¾-1 cup grated meat.

The milk. For fresh coconut milk, place grated coconut in flour sack towel or several layers of cheesecloth and squeeze hard over bowl. You'll get about ¾ cup milk per coconut.

Which Coconut?

Fresh: For confections and Southeast Asian and Chamorro dishes. Also, whenever unsweetened coconut is called for.

Angel flake (flaked, dehydrated, sweetened coconut): For confections.

Dehydrated, unsweetened coconut: Often found in health food stores. For use in confections such as macaroons; combine with coconut milk when moist texture is needed.

Coconut juice or water: The liquid in the center of the coconut; when chilled, a refreshing drink. Some people use it to extend coconut milk.

Coconut milk: The expressed "milk" of coconut juice. May be manually or mechanically pressed. Lite versions, with less fat, are available.

Haupia/Coconut Cornstarch Custard

2 (14 ½ oz.) cans coconut milk

1 (14 oz.) can sweetened condensed milk

Pinch salt

4 ½ Tbsp. cornstarch

4 ½ Tbsp. water

½ c. sweetened, flaked coconut, divided

©iStockphoto.com/Tootles

In saucepan, combine milks; whisk well to combine. Stir in salt. Cook over medium-high heat just until lightly steaming and bubbling at edge. Meanwhile, make a slurry of cornstarch and water, whisking together in bowl or measuring cup. Whisk cornstarch slurry into milk mixture; cook briefly until thickened. Stir in ¼ cup flaked coconut. Pour into serving dish; top with remaining flaked coconut. Serve immediately. Sweet and rich!

Serves 6 to 8

As we make it today, *haupia* is far from the Hawaiian version. The original was made by combining coconut milk or young, soft coconut with grated *pia* (arrowroot) then steaming it in bundles in the *imu* (earth oven). Its texture was most likely that of cream cheese, while many of today's *haupia* puddings have a consistency more like gelatin.

This version, featuring sweetened condensed milk, was a popular early twentieth-century treat among Islander. It's more of a custard, and it tastes best when served hot. Make it right before your dinner party, then place the serving dish in a hot water bath to keep it warm. Serve right after dinner, perhaps draped over a plain vanilla cake or atop broiled pineapple or fresh tropical fruit.

Island Sugar

Sweet Endings

*F*or a couple of generations, Hawai'i was the sugar capital of the world, and a good portion of the population worked on sugar plantations. At one point, plantation workers brought their cloth bags to the mill for their monthly allotment of free sugar.

To this day, we have an extraordinarily sweet palate, and no potluck or party is complete without an array of desserts. Not surprisingly, coconut, pineapple, and other tropical fruits are prominently featured.

©iStockphoto.com/Richard Waller

Uakea Road Sundaes

Guava jelly

Coconut ice cream or gelato

Coconut candy*

In saucepan, over medium-low heat, melt ¼ cup guava jelly per serving. Place scoop of coconut ice cream or gelato in serving dish. Pour jelly over ice cream; top with a scattering of coconut candy.

Serves 1; increase as needed for multiple servings.

No guava jelly?
Use strawberry, raspberry, or other jelly.

No coconut ice cream?
Use vanilla.

To make coconut candy: Crack and shell one coconut; dig out meat. Using a vegetable peeler, shave coconut meat into thin shreds. (Unless you're a perfectionist, there's no need to peel away brown skin.) In rimmed baking pan, arrange coconut in a single layer. Scatter turbinado sugar (brown sugar crystals) over coconut in relatively equal portions of coconut to sugar. Set oven to lowest possible temperature; place baking pan in oven. Bake, periodically stirring and spooning melting sugar over coconut, for 12 to 15 hours (yes, hours!), until coconut is golden brown and candied. Store in airtight container.

My husband and I honeymooned in remote Hāna, Maui. During the long drive there, we couldn't resist the temptation to stop and pick guavas. When we came to Nāhiku (just beyond the halfway point of our journey), we couldn't resist the crispy ribbons of golden-brown candied coconut sold by a man named Willie, who generously shared his technique with us.

Our condo had just enough cooking equipment for a rather primitive round of jelly making, so I dispatched my husband to fetch sugar and cheesecloth from the famous Hasegawa General Store. Rather than cheesecloth to filter the guava juice, the folks at Hasegawa suggested plastic window screening, which worked beautifully. That evening, after boiling guava jelly, we invented this decadent dessert named after the main road through Hāna. Uakea means white rain, referring to the misty rain that often washes through this beautiful part of the world.

Grandma's Old-Fashioned Coconut Pie

3 Tbsp. cornstarch

1 ½ c. water,* divided

3 c. fresh grated, packed coconut

2 c. sugar

½ c. butter, softened

¼ c. flour

¼ tsp. salt

1 tsp. vanilla

8- or 9-inch unbaked double-crust pie crust

In small bowl or measuring cup, whisk together cornstarch and ½ cup water. In medium bowl, combine cornstarch mixture, 1 cup water, coconut, sugar, butter, flour, salt, and vanilla. Mix well. Line pie plate with unbaked pastry. Pour in coconut mixture; top with crust, flute edges, and cut steam vents into pastry. Bake at 375 degrees for 45 minutes.

Serves 8

Variation: For a more intense coconut flavor, use ¾ cup coconut milk and ¾ cup water.

No fresh coconut?
Use 3 cups of sweetened angel flake coconut in place of fresh coconut and omit sugar from the recipe.

Although coconut cream pie is well known today, during my childhood, coconut pies and turnovers were made from fresh coconut rather than the dehydrated, sweetened stuff, and were firmly packed without custard or cream. A thin slice was enough to satisfy the most demanding sweet tooth.

Shortcut coconut cake: Prepare a yellow cake mix according to package directions, but substitute coconut milk for water called for in recipe. To make frosting, cream 4 tablespoons butter with 8 ounces cream cheese, gradually adding 2 teaspoons milk. Beat in 3 ½ cups sifted powdered sugar and ½ teaspoon vanilla. Stir in 2 cups angel flake coconut. Frost cake. Scatter toasted coconut over cake.

Halo Halo/Filipino Parfait

1 box fruit gelatin, any flavor (we like strawberry Jell-O)

3 c. diced fruit—mango, melon, ripe pear, banana, papaya, etc.

1 (12 oz.) jar makapuno (coconut sport, optional)

1 c. half-and-half or whole milk

1 pt. vanilla ice cream, softened (light ice cream is fine)

Sugar or honey to taste (optional)

2 c. crushed ice*

Several hours (or the night before) serving, prepare gelatin using only half the water called for in recipe. Pour into 8-by-8-inch baking dish. Chill. When firm, cut into cubes. In large bowl, combine gelatin cubes, diced fruit, makapuno, half-and-half, and ice cream. Taste and sweeten, as desired. Layer fruit mixture and crushed ice in tall parfait glasses. Serve immediately.

Serves 6 to 8

*See 'Ōkole Maluna chapter, p. 15, for tips on how to make crushed ice.

In the Tagalog dialect of the Philippines, "halo" means to mix, and this crazy, mixed-up dessert is a Filipino favorite. Its components vary widely—it's one of those dishes in which your definition of what it should include depends on how your mother made it. There are key components, however: cut or shredded fruit (even canned fruit cocktail is acceptable); makapuno (coconut sport); something gelatinous (tapioca, gelatin, even rice flour dumplings); something creamy (milk, ice cream, evaporated milk); and crushed ice, all layered in a tall glass just before serving.

Coconut Shortbread

1 c. flour

1 c. sugar

½ c. sweetened flaked coconut

½ tsp. salt

¾ c. cold butter, in eight slices

1 tsp. vanilla

Preheat oven to 350 degrees. In bowl of food processor, combine flour, sugar, coconut, and salt; process briefly to combine. Place butter and vanilla in bowl of food processor; pulse on and off just until mixture resembles small peas. Do not run processor constantly, and do not allow dough to form a ball or become smooth and incorporated. Place mixture in 8-by-8, 9-by-9, or 7-by-11-inch baking dish. Press lightly with fingers or back of spoon to even the surface.

Bake 30 to 40 minutes, until golden brown around edges. Watch carefully—shortbread can burn quickly. Transfer to a rack; cut while still hot using a sharp, thin-bladed knife; wipe knife between slices. Allow to cool before serving.

Serves 24

Tip: To toast coconut, place in nonstick frying pan over high heat. Stir or toss for 3 to 5 minutes until golden. Watch carefully, as it can burn quickly.

If you have a food processor, this very rich, buttery, melting shortbread is ridiculously easy to make. For a special dinner, serve slim fingers of shortbread with vanilla ice cream and a sprinkling of toasted coconut.

©iStockphoto.com/Duncan Walker

Caramel Mochi/Rice Flour Fudge

2 c. sugar

⅔ c. water

1 ¼ tsp. cream of tartar

1 c. heavy cream

1 Tbsp. butter

1 (1 lb.) box mochiko (sweet rice flour), about 3 cups

1 ½ tsp. baking powder

3 eggs, beaten

1 tsp. vanilla

1 c. milk

To make caramel sauce: Boil together sugar, water, and cream of tartar without stirring—but occasionally swirling pot—until dark tan; about 10 minutes. Turn off heat and pour in cream, stirring constantly; it will boil furiously and increase in volume. Remove from heat; stir in butter; set aside to cool.

While caramel sauce is cooking, place rice flour in medium bowl, whisk in baking powder. Stir in eggs and vanilla; stir in milk then cooled caramel sauce. Pour into buttered or oil-sprayed 9-by-13-inch pan. Bake at 350 degrees for 35 to 40 minutes, until a knife inserted in center emerges clean and top is puffed and browned. Cut into small squares.

Serves 24

Butter mochi, a favorite dessert or snack, is very much an Island invention—the marriage of Japanese mochi cakes (pillowy, steamed rice flour confections) and Western-style fudge. It takes many forms in plain, coconut, chocolate, and other versions. This recipe is my invention, flavored with caramel sauce. Butter mochi has a gooey, silky texture and is at its most delicious the day after it's baked. (But who can wait?)

©iStockphoto.com/Thomas Perkins

Pineapple Cream Cheese Pie in No-roll Crust

For crust:

2 c. flour

¼ c. sugar

¼ tsp. salt

½ c. melted butter

2 egg yolks

2 tsp. vanilla

Nonstick spray

In medium bowl, whisk together flour, sugar, and salt. Stir in butter, egg yolks, and vanilla. (Mixture will be dry and a bit crumbly.) Spray 8-inch pie plate with nonstick spray. Lightly press dough into pie plate.

Pie crust has never been my culinary forte, so when I first heard of no-roll crust, I loved the idea. This pie is so easy, and so yummy.

For filling:

8 oz. cream cheese, softened

½ c. brown sugar, packed

1 (20 oz.) can pineapple, in juice, well-drained

1 tsp. vanilla

3 eggs

Dash of salt

Preheat oven to 400 degrees. In medium bowl, combine cream cheese, brown sugar, pineapple, vanilla, eggs, and salt; mix well. Pour into pie crust. Bake 25 to 30 minutes, until pastry is browned and filling is set.

Serves 8

Pineapple Lavender Gelato

1 fresh pineapple, peeled, cored, eyes removed (about 3 cups, chopped)

2 bananas, peeled

¼ c. fresh lime juice (about 2 limes)

¾ c. simple syrup*

1 tsp. ginger juice**

1 c. half-and-half (nonfat is fine)

1 jigger rum

1 tsp. culinary lavender (optional)

Roughly chop pineapple and bananas. In bowl of food processor, combine pineapple, banana, lime juice, simple syrup, ginger juice, half-and-half, rum, and lavender; process until smooth. Correct sweetness. Pour mixture into shallow metal baking pan; freeze until almost solid. Scoop into bowl of food processor; process again until smooth. Place mixture in airtight plastic container, cover, and freeze until solid. Serve in scoops or mounded in dessert dishes. (This mixture freezes quite solid, so remove it from freezer a short time before serving; use ice cream scoop that has been dipped in hot water.)

Serves 10

No culinary lavender? Skip it—the recipe still works.

No fresh pineapple? Use canned crushed pineapple.

To make simple syrup: Place equal parts sugar and water (in this case, ¾ cup each) in a saucepan and bring to a boil, stirring until sugar has dissolved. Cool and use as desired.

**To make ginger juice:* Grate ginger finely, then squeeze to release juice (you can wrap the ginger in cheesecloth if you prefer, but squeezing with your hands is kind of fun).

This dessert marries two ingredients that together represent Hawai'i's agricultural past—pineapple—and its future—lavender. Though not native, pineapple was once our second most important agricultural product, while harvesting of lavender, now grown on several farms at the higher elevations of Maui and the Big Island, began in the 1990s.

If you own an ice cream maker, you can use that instead of the two-step freezing process described in this recipe. On a warm evening, this dessert can also serve as an appetizer or intermezzo.

Asian Pear Cobbler

For the pastry:

1 c. flour

Zest of ½ lemon

½ c. cold butter, cut into pieces

3 Tbsp. sugar

2 Tbsp. cold cream or milk

1 egg

⅛ tsp. salt

In bowl of food processor, combine all pastry ingredients and pulse, on and off, until dough forms a ball and begins to roll around in bowl. Wrap in plastic wrap; refrigerate while you prepare fruit.

For the cobbler:

6 c. sliced Asian pears (peeled or not, as desired);
about 3 large Korean pears; or 4-5 smaller Japanese pears

¼ c. sugar

4 Tbsp. cornstarch

1 Tbsp. Chinese 5-spice

Juice and rind of 1 orange

Butter

No Asian pears?
Use apples
or firm pears.

Preheat oven to 375 degrees. In bowl, toss pears with sugar, cornstarch, and 5-spice powder. Place in buttered 8-by-8-inch baking dish; dot with butter. On floured surface, roll dough out to 8-by-8-inch square. Cover fruit with pastry. Bake until pastry is golden brown and fruit is bubbling, about 25 to 30 minutes.

Serves 8 to 10

Asian pears, the large, exceptionally juicy fruit that resemble a cross between a pear and an apple, came into the U.S. market just a few years back. Though expensive, they offer an irresistibly exotic perfumed flavor and a satisfyingly crisp texture. I wasn't sure how they'd cook, but when I served this cobbler to my brother, he gave it his highest accolade: "It's the bomb, sister!"

147

Svenske in Paradise/Fruit-filled Crêpe

3 eggs, slightly beaten

8 scant Tbsp. sugar

½ tsp. salt

1 c. flour

1 c. milk

3 Tbsp. melted butter or vegetable oil

2 tsp. vanilla, divided

8 oz. cream cheese, softened (regular or lowfat)

¼ c. sugar

2 c. chopped or sliced, well-drained fruit

Vegetable oil or cooking spray

Sweetened whipped cream or crème fraîche for topping

In large bowl, whisk together beaten eggs, sugar, and salt. Place flour in small hand sifter; sift into egg mixture, whisking constantly to prevent lumps. Whisk in milk, fat, and 1 tsp. vanilla. In medium bowl, combine cream cheese, sugar, and fruit. Set aside. Preheat oven to lowest setting. Heat nonstick frying pan over medium-high heat. Place ¼ cup or so of batter in pan; cook until surface goes from shiny to dull; flip and cook until golden with a bit of lacy browning.
Place crêpe on heatproof plate in warm oven. Continue until all crêpes are cooked.

Just before serving, fill warmed crêpes with fruit mixture; top with dollop of whipped cream or crème fraîche.

Serves 6

Variation: Instead of making filling ahead of time, prepare bowls of chopped fruit, sour cream, softened cream cheese, crème fraîche, Mascarpone, chopped nuts, and whatever else sounds good. Cover; set aside. After dinner, invite guests into your kitchen while you fry up crêpes and set up a dessert bar with the prepared ingredients. Let guests fill their own crêpes as they desire.

My Swedish friend, Signe Rea, is a great cook who taught me how to make a number of foolproof recipes that have become regulars in my repertoire. These easy Swedish pancakes, though most often served at breakfast with a filling of lingonberries or a drizzle of maple syrup, are also a sturdy festive dessert. Use any fruit you like, from canned cherries to fresh backyard mango, from crushed pineapple to sliced Asian pears—or feel free to combine different fruits. For a special dinner, make up the batter and refrigerate, then fry just before serving.

Mango (or Peach) Bread Pudding

4 c. whole milk

2 c. stale bread, cubed

½ c. brown sugar, packed

2 c. sliced fresh mango or peaches, well drained

4 Tbsp. cocoa

2 eggs, slightly beaten

½ tsp. salt

1 tsp. vanilla

Butter, softened

Preheat oven to 375 degrees. Pour milk into saucepan; place over medium-high heat. Heat just until small bubbles appear around edge—do not allow to boil. Place cubed bread in large bowl; pour scalded milk over. Allow bread to absorb milk. Gently mix in remaining ingredients. Generously butter casserole or baking dish. Place dish in pan of hot water; pour bread pudding mixture into dish. Bake 1 hour.

Serves 8 to 10

Variation: Although this bread pudding is rich and sweet as it is, if you're in the mood for excess, serve it with a dollop of whipped cream and a drizzle of caramel sauce (either purchased, or the sauce shown within the Caramel Mochi Recipe on p. 143).

Tip: Buy bread a couple of days before you plan to make this recipe; let it harden and dry out. Or dry bread in oven by cutting it into cubes, spreading on cookie sheet and placing in 250-degree oven for 15 minutes.

Islanders just *love* bread pudding. Many Hawai'i bakeries routinely stock squares of firm bread pudding in the pastry case, which is something you don't see on the U.S. mainland. For this recipe, use a substantial country-style artisanal loaf (white or whole wheat). A touch of cocoa and brown sugar gives this version an especially rich flavor.

adobo (ah-doh-boh): Pork and/or chicken braised in tangy soy sauce and vinegar mixture. Philippines.

'ahi (ah-hee): Big-eye or yellowfin tuna.

Asian pears: Round, crisp, juicy, perfumed fruit from Japan, China, or Korea.

awamori (ah-wah-more-ee): Distilled rice liquor unique to Okinawa.

bean threads: Noodles made from mung bean starch, such as sai fun, cellophane noodles, glass noodles. China.

bao (bow—as in bow-wow): Steamed buns made from wheat flour, stuffed with sweet or savory ingredients. China.

bulgogi (bull-go-kee): Barbecued spare ribs. Korea.

Chinese 5-spice: Spice of equal parts cinnamon, cloves, fennel, star anise, and Szechuan peppercorn.

coconut sport: tender coconut spoon-meat, sold in jars in Asian groceries.

daikon (dye-con): White radish. Japan.

dashi (dah-shee): Delicately flavored fish broth made from dried seaweed and shaved bonito tuna. Japan

edamame (ay-dah-mah-may): Green soybeans; sold both fresh and frozen, in the shell and shelled; favorite snack food in Japanese taverns.

furikake (foo-ree-kah-kay): A family of seasoning mixtures using shreds of dried seaweed and such flavoring ingredients as sesame seeds, salt, and chiles. Japan.

haupia (how-pee-ah): Coconut pudding or custard. Hawai'i.

Hawaiian salt: Salt flakes; the nearest substitute is kosher salt.

hiyayakko (hee-yah-yah-ko): Cold tofu drizzled with sauce; a favorite tavern food in Japan.

hoisin (hoy-sin): a thick, sweet, salty, and spicy soybean-based sauce. China.

'inamona (ee-nah-mow-nah): A relish of roasted, ground *kukui* nuts (candlenuts) and Hawaiian salt, often with fresh or dried chiles added. Hawai'i.

jasmine rice: Fragrant long-grain rice favored by Southeast Asians.

jook (juk): Rice gruel also known as congee (kohn-jay). China.

kalo (kah-low): Taro, the staple food of Hawaiians. There are wetland varieties, which are grown in paddies, like rice, and dryland varieties. The former are grown for the corm, the potato-like tuber that is steamed, ground, and pounded to make poi. The latter provides the large, heart-shaped leaves, called lū'au leaves, which, when boiled, become a spinach-like vegetable invariably served at feasts. Taro is extremely nutritious and readily digested.

kālua (kah-loo-ah): To bake, generally in the earth oven called an *imu*; *kālua* pork is a lū'au staple. Hawai'i.

katsuoboshi (kah-tsoo-oh-bow-shee): Dried bonito (tuna) shaved into flakes; one of two ingredients essential to making the Japanese stock called dashi.

kombu (comb-boo): Kelp; a mild-flavored gray-to-black seaweed sold in dried sheets; one of two essential ingredients for making the stock called dashi. Japan.

kukui (koo-koo-ee) nuts: The oily nut of the candlenut tree, Aleurites moluccana, so called because the pressed oil was used to make primitive lanterns. The nuts are roasted and ground for the popular relish *'inamona*; however, eating too much *kukui* is notorious for causing loose bowels. Hawai'i.

laulau (pronounced like "how-how"): Packet of ti leaves stuffed with meat, fish, and vegetables; steamed in an earth oven. Hawai'i.

lomi (low-mee) salmon: In Hawaiian, to "*lomi*" means to massage. *Lomi* salmon is a condiment or salad made from salt salmon massaged with the fingers to break it into bite-size pieces.

long rice: See bean threads.

lū'au (loo-ow): A Hawaiian feast.

lū'au leaf: The leaf of the taro plant. Hawai'i.

matsutake (mah-tsoo-tah-kay): A highly prized mushroom. Japan.

mirin (mee-reen): A sweet seasoning; sweet rice wine. Japan.

miso (mee-soh): Salty fermented soybean paste. Japan.

mochi rice, mochi flour (moh-chee): Ground rice flour. Japan

namasu (nah-mah-sue): Vinegared dish of raw vegetables and, sometimes, seafood. Japan.

nīoi (nee-oy): Small, red, hot chiles. Hawai'i.

nori (noh-rhee): Dried black seaweed. Japan.

okazu (oh-zah-koo): Japanese-style delicatessen.

panko (pan-koh): Breading. Japan.

patis (pah-teese): Fish sauce. Philippines.

piri-piri (pee-ree pee-ree): Chile relish. Portugal.

poi (poy): Steamed, mashed, fermented paste of taro corm. Hawai'i.

poke (poh-kay): Raw fish relish; with seaweed, various sauces. Hawai'i.

rafute (rah-foo-tay): Braised pork. Okinawa.

sake (sah-kay): Rice wine. Japan.

sambal oelek (sahm-bahl oh-lek): Chile and garlic relish. Indonesia.

sesame oil: Raw or roasted oil of sesame seeds.

shiitake (shee-tah-kay): Mushrooms; often dried and reconstituted in warm water before use. Japan.

shoyu (shoh-you): Soy sauce. Japan.

sinigang (sin-ih-gahng): Tamarind sweet-sour soup. Philippines.

sriracha (shree-rah-chah): Hot sauce. Thailand.

tamarind: Bulbous bean pod of the tamarind tree; when peeled and seeded, used to create a piquant sour flavor in soups, stews, sauces, beverages.

taro (tah-row): Colocasia esculenta; centerpiece food of Hawaiian diet, with all parts eaten—leaf, corm, flowers.

ti (tee): Leaf of the Cordyline terminalis; used as wrapper, plate, décor, and lei in Hawai'i.

tofu (toh-foo): Soybean curd; available soft or firm. Japan.

wasabi (wah-sah-bee): A type of horseradish. Japan.

Index